# LEARNING FROM IRAQ: COUNTERINSURGENCY IN AMERICAN STRATEGY

**Steven Metz**

**January 2007**

*****

The views expressed in this report are those of the author and do not necessarily reflect the official policy or position of the Department of the Army, the Department of Defense, or the U.S. Government. This report is cleared for public release; distribution is unlimited.

****

The author would like to thank Lieutenant General Peter Chiarelli, Lieutenant General David Petraeus, Frank Hoffman, T. X. Hammes, John Martin, Dr. Antulio Echevarria, Dr. Conrad Crane, Dr. Andrew Terrill, Colonel Trey Braun, Lincoln Krause, and Lieutenant Colonel Raymond Millen for insights or helpful comments on earlier drafts of this monograph. All remaining shortcomings are, of course, strictly those of the author and persist despite the best efforts of this cadre of experts. This monograph is dedicated to those who lost their lives or their youth in Iraq, and those who worked hard to prevent this.

*****

Comments pertaining to this report are invited and should be forwarded to: Director, Strategic Studies Institute, U.S. Army War College, 122 Forbes Ave, Carlisle, PA 17013-5244.

*****

All Strategic Studies Institute (SSI) publications are available on the SSI homepage for electronic dissemination. Hard copies of this report also may be ordered from our homepage. SSI's homepage address is: www.StrategicStudiesInstitute.army.mil.

*****

The Strategic Studies Institute publishes a monthly e-mail newsletter to update the national security community on the research of our analysts, recent and forthcoming publications, and upcoming conferences sponsored by the Institute. Each newsletter also provides a strategic commentary by one of our research analysts. If you are interested in receiving this newsletter, please subscribe on our homepage at www.StrategicStudiesInstitute.army.mil/newsletter/.

ISBN 1-58487-272-1

# FOREWORD

During the past 5 years, American strategy has undergone a sea change, shifting from a focus on the conventional military forces of rogue or rising states to irregular challenges associated with the "long war" against transnational jihadism. Much of the new thinking has resulted from the conflict in Iraq.

One result of this has been an attempt to relearn counterinsurgency by the U.S. military. While the involvement of the United States in counterinsurgency has a long history, it had faded in importance in the years following the end of the Cold War. When American forces first confronted it in Iraq, they were not fully prepared. Since then, the U.S. military and other government agencies have expended much effort to refine their counterinsurgency capabilities. But have they done enough?

In this monograph, Dr. Steven Metz, who has been writing on counterinsurgency for several decades, draws strategic lessons about counterinsurgency from the Iraq conflict. He contends that the United States is likely to undertake it in coming decades but, based on the performance in Iraq, may not be adequately prepared depending on the grand strategy which the United States adopts.

The Strategic Studies Institute is pleased to offer this monograph as a contribution to Army and Joint thinking about the conflict in Iraq and, more broadly, about U.S. strategy for the "long war."

DOUGLAS C. LOVELACE, JR.
Director
Strategic Studies Institute

iii

# BIOGRAPHICAL SKETCH OF THE AUTHOR

STEVEN METZ is Chairman of the Regional Strategy and Planning Department and Research Professor of National Security Affairs at the Strategic Studies Institute (SSI). He has been with SSI since 1993, previously serving as Henry L. Stimson Professor of Military Studies and SSI's Director of Research. Dr. Metz has also been on the faculty of the Air War College, the U.S. Army Command and General Staff College, and several universities. He has been an advisor to political campaigns and elements of the intelligence community; served on security policy task forces; testified in both houses of Congress; and spoken on military and security issues around the world. He is the author of more than 100 publications on national security, military strategy, and world politics. Since 2003, he has concentrated on the Iraq conflict. He is currently serving on the RAND Corporation's Insurgency Board and is at work on two books: *Iraq and the Evolution of American Strategy* and *Insurgency and Counterinsurgency in the 21st Century*, both scheduled for publication in 2007. Dr. Metz holds a B.A. in Philosophy and a M.A. in International Studies from the University of South Carolina, and a Ph.D. in Political Science from the Johns Hopkins University.

# SUMMARY

When the United States removed Saddam Hussein from power in the spring of 2003, American policymakers and military leaders did not expect to become involved in a protracted counterinsurgency campaign in Iraq. But it has now become the seminal conflict of the current era and will serve as a paradigm for future strategic decisions.

The United States has a long history of involvement in irregular conflict. During the Cold War, this took the form of supporting friendly regimes against communist-based insurgents. After the Cold War, though, the military assumed that it would not undertake protracted counterinsurgency and did little develop its capabilities for this type of conflict. Then the terrorist attacks of September 11, 2001, forced President Gorege W. Bush and his top advisers to reevaluate the global security environment and American strategy. The new strategy required the United States to replace regimes which support terrorism or help bring ungoverned areas which terrorists might use as sanctuary under control. Under some circumstances, such actions could involve counterinsurgency. Iraq was a case in point. It has forced the U.S. military to relearn counterinsurgency on the fly.

Since the summer of 2003, the conflict in Iraq has taken the form of a deadly learning game between the insurgents and the counterinsurgents (both U.S. and Iraqi forces). By 2006, it had evolved from resistance to the American presence to a complex war involving sectarian militias, Iraqi and American security forces, foreign jihadists, and Sunni Arab insurgents. While, by that point, the United States had refined its counterinsurgency strategy, this may have come too late. In addition, the conflict was placing great stress on the military, particularly the Army.

The Iraq conflict reinforced what national security specialists long have known: the United States is adept at counterinsurgency support in a limited role but faces serious, even debilitating challenges when developing and implementing a comprehensive counterinsurgency strategy for a partner state. Most policymakers, military leaders, and defense analysts, though, believe that American involvement in counterinsurgency is inevitable as the "long war" against jihadism unfolds. This means that the United States needs a strategy and an organization that can conduct counterinsurgency effectively. Since 2003, the Department of Defense has undertaken a number of reforms to augment effectiveness at counterinsurgency and other irregular operations.

Whether these are adequate or not depends on future grand strategy. If counterinsurgency does remain a central element of American strategy and the United States elects to play a central or dominant role in it, the current reforms might be inadequate. If, on the other hand, the United States chose to optimize its capability for counterinsurgency it would need an organization which is:

- intelligence-centric;
- fully interagency and, if possible, multinational at every level;
- capable of rapid response;
- capable of sustained, high-level involvement in a protracted operation;
- capable of seamless integration with partners;

- culturally and psychologically adept; and,
- capable of organizational, conceptual and tactical adjustment "on the fly."

Ultimately, the United States might need to jettison the concept of counterinsurgency in favor of the broader concept of stabilization and transformation operations. This would help clarify strategy and priorities. In particular, it would reinforce the idea that military force is a secondary factor in counterinsurgency. It is not warfighting simply against irregular enemies.

In the final reckoning, the U.S. effort in Iraq has had a number of problems. We used flawed strategic assumptions, did not plan adequately, and had a doctrinal void. There was a mismatch between strategic ends and means applied to them. By signaling in advance that we would go so far and no further, by taking escalation off the table in the insurgency's early months, we made it easier for the insurgents to convince themselves and their supporters that their ability to weather punishment outstrips the willingness of the United States to impose it. By failing to prepare for counterinsurgency in Iraq and by failing to avoid it, the United States has increased the chances of facing it again in the near future. We did not establish security before attempting transformation, thus allowing the insurgency to reach a point of psychological "set" which was difficult to reverse fairly quickly. Linking the conflict in Iraq to the global war on terror skewed the normal logic of strategy. By approaching counterinsurgency as a type of warfighting during its first year, we reverted to a strategy of attrition which did not work.

Whether Iraq ultimately turns into a success or failure, it is invaluable as a source of illumination for American strategy. If it is a unique occurrence then once it is settled, the U.S. military can return to its old, conventionally-focused trajectory of transformation. But if Iraq is a portent of the future — if protracted, ambiguous, irregular, cross-cultural, and psychologically complex conflicts are to be the primary mission of the future American military (and the other, equally important parts of the U.S. security organization) — then serious change must begin.

# LEARNING FROM IRAQ: COUNTERINSURGENCY IN AMERICAN STRATEGY

The world is grown so bad
That wrens make prey where eagles dare not perch.

William Shakespeare
*Richard III*

## The Deadly Bloom.

The defining conflict of our time never was supposed to happen. American policymakers expected a warm welcome for U.S. forces in Iraq. The Iraqi people, they believed, would be grateful for liberation.[1] Iraq would move quickly toward a democratic political system and open economy. Expatriates would provide new leadership untainted—or at least less tainted—by Hussein. Iraq's own police and military would secure the country. Because the U.S. military had used precision strikes to limit damage during the march on Baghdad, recovery would be fast. Iraqi oil revenues would fund reconstruction. Nongovernmental organizations (NGOs) and the international community—once they overcame their pique at the intervention—would provide money, expertise, and peacekeepers. Iraq's neighbors, relieved at having a cancer removed from their midst, would help or at least stay out of the way. Stabilizing and rebuilding Iraq, American policymakers believed, would be easier than removing Hussein.

Unfortunately, events did not follow script. As soon as the old regime was destroyed, Iraq collapsed in a

1

nation-wide spasm of looting and street crime. The Iraqi security forces disappeared. With nothing to take their place, violence ran unchecked. The anarchy sparked public anger which grew into a storm, gathering energy with passing weeks. For a brief interlude, little of the violence was directed against the American forces.[2] But that did not last long. Trouble first broke out in the restive city of Fallujah, 35 miles west of Baghdad.[3] Fallujah was insular, conservative, intensely religious, and resistant to outside control, attracting radical clerics like moths to a flame. It was a traditional hotbed of smuggling and a city where complex tribal connections mattered greatly, helping define personal loyalty, obligation, and honor. Even Saddam Hussein largely had left the place alone. It was bypassed in the original assault on Baghdad, but elements of the 82d Airborne Division arrived in late April 2003. The citizens did not take kindly to occupation. Within a few days, a rally celebrating Saddam Hussein's birthday led to angry denunciations of the U.S. presence and heated demands for withdrawal. Shooting broke out, leaving at least 13 Iraqis dead.[4] Two more died the next day in a second round of clashes.[5] Attackers then tossed grenades into a U.S. Army compound.[6] Without drawing a moral comparison, Fallujah was like Lexington and Concord — an inadvertent clash that funneled discontent toward organized resistance.

Still, the turn to violence was not immediate across Iraq. Frustration grew gradually to a storm-like intensity, faster in some places than others. "Thank you for removing the tyrant," more and more Iraqis concluded, "but now go home." At the same time — and contradictorily — they complained that a nation as powerful as the United States could restore order and public services if it desired, so the failure to do so was punishment intended to dishonor them. Even many who had opposed Hussein believed that intervention was designed to control Iraq's oil and promote Israeli security. Frustration led to anger. Anger began turning violent. At first it was sporadic. In early May two American soldiers were killed in Baghdad, one in a daylight assassination while directing traffic and the other by a sniper.[7] On May 27, two more died during a nighttime attack on an Army checkpoint near Fallujah.[8] Iraq's south appeared quieter but was far from stable. British forces, despite a June incident in the town of Majar al-Kabir which left six military policemen dead, took a more relaxed approach to occupation duties, leaving local religious and militia leaders (and, as it turned out, criminal gangs) to compete for power.[9] In the holy cities of Karbala and Najaf, clerics preserved a fragile order.[10]

In the middle of May, several thousand Shiites marched in Baghdad, demanding an immediate transfer of power to an elected government.[11] Grand Ayatollah Ali Hamid Maqsoon al-Sistani, Iraq's senior Shiite cleric, issued a fatwa condemning the idea of a constitutional council named by the American occupation authority, saying Iraqis should draft their own constitution.[12] But the most worrisome development in the Shiite areas was the emergence of Moqtada al-Sadr, son of an esteemed cleric killed by Hussein who was gaining fervent supporters, especially in Basra and the sprawling slum on the east side of Baghdad. He quickly discovered that opposing the Americans (along with the social services programs his organization operated) built support among the Shiite lower classes.[13] As often happens during times of political turmoil, extremism trumped moderation in the quest for attention. Controlling Sadr became a persistent and vexing problem.

Elsewhere violence against American forces spread, particularly in Baghdad and cities such as Baqubah, Samarra, Habaniyah, Khaldiya, Fallujah, and Tikrit, and across the region west and north of the capital known as the "Sunni triangle." The initial attacks lacked sophistication, but as more former military members — unemployed by the disbanding of the Iraqi army — joined in, the resistance began to show a greater understanding of guerrilla operations.[14] Armed bands began to focus on vulnerable targets such as isolated checkpoints and slow-moving convoys. Stand-off attacks using rockets and mortars, which allowed the attackers to flee after firing a few rounds, became more frequent.[15] Iraqis who worked for the Americans or were part of the new administrative structure came under attack.[16] Translators were favorite victims. Insurgents sabotaged the electrical grid, water system, and oil pipelines. Like their forebears in earlier insurgencies, the Iraqi resistance fighters understood that a country's rulers — the Americans in this case — were blamed for the lack of water, electricity, and fuel, even though the insurgents themselves were causing the problem. The greater public anger and frustration, the insurgents knew, the better for them.

During the summer a group of Hussein loyalists calling itself al-Awda ("the return") made open overtures to Islamic militants linked to al-Qai'da, while other elements of the resistance sent feelers to leading Shiite clergy.[17] There were reports that former regime officials were recruiting foreign fighters. U.S. forces encountered Syrians, Saudis, Yemenis, Algerians, Lebanese, and Chechens, indicating that the international jihadist network, born in Afghanistan in the 1980s, was turning its attention to Iraq.[18] Capitalizing on the number of unemployed Iraqi men, most with military and police training, and criminals released from prison earlier in the year, Hussein loyalists began paying for the killing of American troops, creating a body of free lance or informal insurgents.[19]

As early as June, some strategic analysts warned that the fighting constituted an organized guerrilla war, not simply the final spasms of the defeated regime.[20] But U.S. officials rejected this idea. Secretary of Defense Donald Rumsfeld attributed the violence to "the remnants of the Ba'ath regime and Fedayeen death squads" and "foreign terrorists" who were "being dealt with in an orderly and forceful fashion by coalition forces."[21] Major General Raymond Odierno, commander of the 4th Infantry Division, described his unit's operations as "daily contact with noncompliant forces, former regime members, and common criminals." "This is not guerrilla warfare," he continued, "it is not close to guerrilla warfare because it's not coordinated, it's not organized, and it's not led."[22] As summer wore on, though, it increasingly was difficult to sustain that argument. Finally, on July 16, General John Abizaid, the new commander of U.S. Central Command (CENTCOM), concluded that the United States was facing "a classical guerrilla type campaign." "It's low-intensity conflict in our doctrinal terms," he said, "but it's war, however you describe it."[23] The optimism of a month earlier, the hope of a quick and relatively painless transition to a post-Hussein Iraq, was gone. As Thomas Ricks put it, the insurgency was in "deadly bloom."[24] The U.S. military thus found itself thrust into a type of conflict it thought it had left behind with the end of the Cold War—counterinsurgency.

From this unexpected beginning, the counter-insurgency campaign in Iraq has produced a lode of tactical and operational lessons. These are vital and invaluable, helping keep American troops alive in a dangerous environment. But the strategic implications are even more enduring. The counterinsurgency campaign in Iraq can only be understood as part — or at least as the logical culmination — of a series of strategic decisions about when and how American power should be used. It shows our strengths and our weaknesses when dealing with such conflicts. Equally important, the campaign will affect future strategic decisions, serving as a catalyst, a driver, and a locomotive. While the outcome in Iraq still hangs in the balance, events there already are shaping the way that policymakers, military leaders, Congress, and the public think about insurgency and the American role in responding to it. The Iraq insurgency, in other words, will become a strategic paradigm. What, then, does it tell us about the role of counterinsurgency in American national security, national defense, and military strategy? How can or should the military react when America's grand strategy places it in a dominant position for a task for which it is not optimized? At the grand strategic level, does the United States want a security apparatus optimized for counterinsurgency? If so, what would this entail?

**The Road to Baghdad.**

The United States has a long history of involvement in irregular conflict. The Indian Wars of the 19th century and interventions in the Philippines, the Caribbean, and Central America in the first part of the 20th gave the American military experience with resistance movements and guerrilla enemies. Modern counterinsurgency began when presidents Harry Truman and Dwight Eisenhower provided support and advice to pro-Western regimes threatened by leftist insurgents. It became a major component of American strategy when President John Kennedy, concerned by Russian leader Nikita Khrushchev's January 1961 speech endorsing "wars of national liberation," the eroding security situation in Laos and South Vietnam, the consolidation of Fidel Castro's regime in Cuba, the French defeat in Algeria, and the outbreak of communist insurgencies in Colombia and Venezuela, became convinced that indirect aggression posed a serious threat to the United States. The idea was that the Soviet Union, blocked from direct aggression against Western Europe, had adopted an indirect strategy, seeking to wear down Washington's will by embroiling it in far-flung internal wars. While any given insurgency might not constitute a risk, in combination they could lead to "death by a thousand small cuts."

Americans respond to new threats or strategic challenges by reorganizing, reforming, and starting new programs. So Kennedy ordered a series of initiatives to improve the counterinsurgency capacity of the military and the government as a whole. He created a cabinet-level Interdepartmental Committee on Overseas Internal Defense Policy to unify counterinsurgency strategy across the disparate elements of the government.[25] The Pentagon established the Office on Counter-Insurgency and Special Activities, giving its director access to the Joint Chiefs of Staff and the Secretary of Defense.[26] The services incorporated counterinsurgency into their professional educational systems and training programs. Army Special Forces expanded and were reoriented toward counterinsurgency. Even the State Department and Agency for International Development got on board, devoting more of their personnel and their budgets to nations facing internal conflict.[27]

Kennedy's reforms were based on the type of counterinsurgency that the United States had undertaken up to that point—providing advice and support to a government facing an indigenous revolutionary movement with external ties. But the "death by a thousand small cuts" idea led the United States into Vietnam even though this was a different type of conflict where Americans assumed the major role, thus turning it into a war of liberation. Sound strategy requires that the costs incurred and risks undertaken in pursuit of a specific policy should be proportional to the expected benefits. By imbuing Vietnam with great symbolism, its perceived strategic significance was skewed far out of proportion to its real importance. This was to be an enduring problem in counterinsurgency: to mobilize and sustain support from Congress and the public, presidents had to portray a conflict as vitally important. But once that perception was established, it was difficult to extricate the United States or diminish the American role, even when the effort was no longer worth its economic or blood costs.

The United States left Vietnam with a vastly improved understanding of insurgency. Or, at least, of the most successful and threatening form of insurgency—Maoist "people's war."[28] It also left the public and the military with a deep distaste for counterinsurgency. Both would probably have preferred that the United States never again undertake it. But in strategy, the enemy "has a vote." Following Vietnam, a series of victories by insurgents backed to one degree or the other by the Soviets—Angola, Mozambique, Nicaragua—made the "death of a thousand small cuts" again seem plausible.

With renewed presidential concern and an active push from a important group of defense specialists in

Congress, counterinsurgency experienced a resurgence throughout the Department of Defense (DoD) and other elements of the U.S. Government during the 1980s, this time as part of a broader category called "low intensity conflict." Special Operations Forces underwent an extensive expansion.[29] Congress created an Assistant Secretary of Defense for Special Operations and Low-Intensity Conflict as well as the United States Special Operations Command (USSOCOM).[30] It urged the National Security Council to form a low-intensity conflict board.[31] The Army's Special Warfare Center, the School of the Americas, and the Air Force's Special Operations School expanded their course offerings. SOCOM created a program on low-intensity conflict at the Naval Postgraduate School. The services developed "proponency offices" to coordinate thinking and education.[32] The Army and Air Force established a Center for Low-Intensity Conflict at Langley Air Force Base near Hampton, Virginia. Army Special Operations Forces and the foreign area officer program grew. The Central Intelligence Agency augmented its covert action capability.[33]

While the Reagan administration was convinced of the need to confront Soviet proxy war, Vietnam suggested that the United States needed a different approach. The small Central American nation of El Salvador became the laboratory. For the U.S. military, this was a chance to "get counterinsurgency right." According to an important 1988 assessment prepared by four Army lieutenant colonels, "El Salvador represents an experiment, an attempt to reverse the record of American failure in waging small wars, an effort to defeat an insurgency by providing training and material support without committing American troops to combat."[34] U.S. military advisors were determined that El Salvador would not become "another Vietnam." Armed with "lessons" from Southeast Asia, they urged the El Salvador Armed Forces (ESAF) to stress pacification, civil defense, and population security rather than the destruction of guerrilla units. The military, American experts believed, should operate in small units with strict constraints on the use of firepower. Since support from the population was the crux of counterinsurgency, military activities were subordinate to economic, political, and psychological ones. Unlike Vietnam, the American footprint was kept small. By law, the United States was to have no more than 55 military personnel in El Salvador at any given time.[35] The primary tools of American policy were advice and assistance. Military aid peaked at $196.6 million in 1984, economic assistance at $462.9 million in 1987.[36] By the end of the 1980s, El Salvador was a democracy—albeit a fragile one—the ESAF was reasonably proficient, and the insurgents stood little chance of victory. A January 1992 peace accord ended the conflict and integrated the insurgents back into Salvadoran life and its political system.

From this experience, the "El Salvador" model of counterinsurgency gained advocates. As debate over the appropriate American strategy in Iraq grew in recent years, some counterinsurgency specialists proposed a variant of the "light footprint" approach used in El Salvador. What this overlooks, though, are four factors which limit the extent to which the "El Salvador" model can be applied to other insurgencies: 1) El Salvador's location made it easier to convince the public and Congress that the United States had a direct stake in the outcome of the conflict; 2) Congress' pressure on the Reagan administration concerning human rights abuses made El Salvador's political and military leaders believe that in the absence of significant reform, Washington would abandon them. In other words, the perception that the United States was willing to write El Salvador off to the insurgents if necessary made its regime more open to the types of deep reforms necessary to undercut the root causes of the conflict; 3) the United States provided an extremely high level of assistance to the Salvadoran government, thus allowing it to undertake significant improvements in its security forces as well as numerous economic development projects; and, 4) El Salvador's culture was Western, and thus social, economic, and political reform readily took root.

Still, El Salvador was heralded within the military as a model. The Army and Air Force codified the counterinsurgency experience of Vietnam by way of El Salvador with the 1990 release of Field Manual (FM) 100-20/ Air Force Manual (AFM) 3-20, *Military Operations in Low-Intensity Conflict*. Success in low-intensity conflict, according to this doctrine, is based on five "imperatives": political dominance, unity of effort, adaptability, legitimacy, and perseverance.[37] The pivotal concept is legitimacy defined in a Western, rationalistic framework. The assumption was that people would support either the insurgents or the government based on an assessment of which side was likely to offer them the best deal in terms of goods and services, whether political goods like civil rights or tangible goods like schools and roads. Under the internal defense and development (IDAD) strategy, the partner government "identifies the genuine grievances of its people and takes political, economic, and social actions to redress them."[38] The role of the U.S. military was to provide support to the partner regime, not to design and lead the counterinsurgency campaign.

This would "normally center on security assistance program administration." Direct involvement of U.S. forces "will be rare." Other Army doctrine stated, "The introduction of US combat forces into an insurgency to conduct counterguerrilla operations is something that is done when all other US and host country responses have been inadequate. US combat forces are never the first units into a country. They are normally the last."[39]

However sound this approach, insurgency evoked little concern in Washington after the downfall of the Soviet Union.[40] Counterinsurgency remained in doctrine but, since it no longer served as proxy war between the superpowers, its role in American strategy was minimal. As a result, the military made little effort to prepare for it. It was a forgotten art — or at least a nearly forgotten one, remembered mostly by the previous generation of experts and a tiny handful of serving officers, most in the Special Forces.[41] American involvement in internal wars took the form of multinational peacekeeping rather than counterinsurgency. For the post-Cold War U.S. military, conventional combat in Operation DESERT STORM and multinational peacekeeping in the Balkans were defining events. Most of the military (as well as significant segments of the public and Congress) subscribed to the idea that armed force should only be used when vital national interests were at stake, when the military objectives were clear, the commitment close ended, and — importantly — when force could be applied in an overwhelming fashion.[42]

By the end of the 1990s, though, some military leaders and defense experts were raising the idea that America's prowess in high-tech conventional war meant that no enemy would attempt it. Instead they would use what DoD began calling "asymmetric" methods.[43] Explicit mention of asymmetry first appeared in joint doctrine in 1995 albeit in a simplistic and limited sense.[44] Doctrine defined asymmetric engagements as those between dissimilar forces, specifically air versus land, air versus sea, and so forth.[45] The 1995 *National Military Strategy* approached the issue more broadly, listing terrorism, the use or threatened use of weapons of mass destruction (WMD), and information warfare as asymmetric challenges. In 1997, the concept of asymmetric threat began to receive greater attention. That year's *Quadrennial Defense Review* stated, "U.S. dominance in the conventional military arena may encourage adversaries to use . . . asymmetric means to attack our forces and interests overseas and Americans at home."[46] The National Defense Panel (NDP), a senior level group commissioned by Congress to provide an assessment of the long-term defense issues the United States faced, was even more explicit. The Panel's report stated:

> We can assume that our enemies and future adversaries have learned from the Gulf War. They are unlikely to confront us conventionally with mass armor formations, air superiority forces, and deep-water naval fleets of their own, all areas of overwhelming U.S. strength today. Instead, they may find new ways to attack our interests, our forces, and our citizens. They will look for ways to match their strengths against our weaknesses.[47]

Following this, there was a flurry of activity to flesh out the meaning and implications of strategic asymmetry, particularly within the intelligence community and the Joint Staff.[48] The most important internal study within DoD was the 1999 Joint Strategy Review, *Asymmetric Approaches to Warfare*.

The idea that the United States should shift its strategy to asymmetric threats, though, was never accepted fully by a military and defense community focused on, even wedded to, high tech conventional war. There were many discussions and admissions, but few changes to programs, organizations, or, most importantly, the defense budget. *Joint Vision 2010*, a 1995 document prepared by the Chairman to provide a "conceptual template" for the future development of the U.S. Armed Forces did not even mention asymmetric threats.[49] *Joint Vision 2020*, the follow-on document released in 2000, did, but focused on the acquisition of high technology like ballistic missiles by America's enemies (without fully explaining why that was "asymmetric"). Finally, the Secretary of Defense's Annual Report to Congress in 1998 and 1999 noted that U.S. dominance in the conventional military arena encourages adversaries to seek asymmetric means of attacking U.S. military forces, U.S. interests, and Americans. The 2000 Annual Report, dropped the word "asymmetric."

To some extent, though, President Bill Clinton did refocus DoD and other elements of the government on low end challenges. Shaping the security environment through military engagement, humanitarian intervention, peacekeeping, and nation-building was nearly the equal of conventional warfighting in the Clinton strategy. But President George W. Bush entered office, vowing to reverse this. Embroiling the U.S. military in such activities, he felt, frittered away its warfighting strength and drew off resources needed for defense transformation. The U.S. military, he had stated during a 1999 campaign speech, "needs the rallying point of a defining mission. And that mission is to deter wars—and win wars when deterrence fails. Sending our military on vague, aimless and endless deployments is the swift solvent of morale."[50]

Condoleezza Rice, one of Governor Bush's primary national security advisers during the 2000 election campaign, wrote, "The president must remember that the military is a special instrument. It is lethal, and it is meant to be. It is not a civilian police force. It is not a political referee. And it is most certainly not designed to build a civilian society."[51]

In the early months of the Bush presidency, China and missile defense dominated the strategic agenda. Then the terrorist attacks of September 2001 forced Bush and his top advisers to reevaluate the global security environment and American strategy. September 11 showed that globalization and connectivity had created a world where problems far away, whether outright conflict or bad governance, could endanger not only U.S. interests in the part of the world where these things occurred, but the security of the American homeland as well. Suddenly political repression, poverty, state failure, and internal conflict, even in far away places, mattered deeply. The question was what to do about it. Neither the Cold War strategic paradigm which viewed regional conflicts as proxy superpower competition nor the post-Cold War paradigm based on a leading role for the United Nations (UN) and a strategic division of labor with allies and partners applied.

Before September 11, American grand strategy had been based on a tightly constrained strategic role for armed force. During the Cold War, war plans sought to restore the status quo ante bellum as rapidly as possible rather than re-engineering the political order, in large part to avoid escalation which might lead to nuclear armageddon. With the end of the Cold War, America's strategic objectives remained limited, in part because the national interests at stake in most conflicts were modest and in part because Presidents George H.

W. Bush and Clinton remained concerned about the willingness of the American public and its elected leaders to support costly or protracted military operations. Moreover, the fact that most post-Cold War military operations took place within a multinational context also limited U.S. strategic objectives. The broader a coalition, the more difficult it is to get all of its members to agree. The normal solution was a "lowest common denominator" approach, with limited strategic objectives.

Following September 11, the United States adopted a more expansive and aggressive grand strategy, with an expanded role for military power. "We must take the battle to the enemy," President Bush said, "disrupt his plans, and confront the worst threats before they emerge. In the world we have entered, the only path to safety is the path of action."[52] This idea carried immense strategic implications. Unless the underlying causes of instability and aggression were removed, aggression eventually would reappear. The Bush strategy thus sought to ameliorate or eradicate the causes of instability and aggression, preferably with, but if necessary without, a broad coalition and the explicit approval of the UN. Removing regimes which either undertook direct aggression or allowed their territory to be used for aggression was the easiest part of the new strategy, in part because the U.S. military was configured for regime take-down. The problem was stabilizing and transforming nations after a regime was removed or collapsed.

Stabilizing and transforming a state is extremely complex, nearly always taking many years or even decades. It demands a comprehensive knowledge of the culture, history, and regional context of the state in question. Most of the work does not involve armed conflict, so in a perfect world, militaries would focus on those tasks which did require force and leave the rest to nonmilitary organizations. In reality, militaries often are the only organizations with the capacity for complex missions in unstable environments, so they often end up playing a major role. The U.S. military, for instance, led the way in Somalia, Haiti, the Balkans, Rwanda, Cambodia, and elsewhere. But with exception of Somalia, these operations took place in situations which were dangerous and complex, but not overtly hostile. The U.S. military was able to shift mentally from warfighting to stabilization. Yet it was never asked to be warfighters, stabilizers, and transformers simultaneously, at least not for an extended period of time in the face of sustained resistance. But that was the old world.

Throughout 2002, the Bush administration wrestled with the question of how to deal with Saddam Hussein, the Iraqi dictator who had destabilized the vital Southwest Asia region and threatened important U.S. national interests for decades. When the President opted to remove Hussein from power in March 2003, the U.S. military executed a masterful campaign, crushing the Iraqi army and seizing Baghdad in a few weeks.[53] But the administration's objectives were not simply to remove Hussein, but to engineer a new Iraq which would not threaten its neighbors, pursue WMD, or support terrorists. In an even larger sense, President Bush sought to use Iraq as a catalyst to unleash political and economic reform in the Islamic world which, he hoped, would alter the conditions which gave rise to jihadism. Unfortunately, some Iraqis, particularly Sunni Arabs and others tied to the Hussein regime, had different goals.

**We Planned for the Wrong Contingency.**

There is a revolutionary slogan attributed to Vladimir Lenin that states, "the worse, the better." When attempting to overthrow a strong regime, it suggests, any action which causes disorder and undercuts public trust in the state is useful. Every insurgency must both destroy the old system and fill the power and security vacuum itself. Insurgent strategies such as the one developed by Mao Zedong saw these two processes as simultaneous or, at least, overlapping. Maoists attempted to destroy the old and create the new at the same time. An insurgent strategy of "mayhem," by contrast, focuses solely on destroying the old system with the hope that whatever ensues will be better. It is the strategic equivalent of shooting blindly into the dark rather than aiming for a specific target. Such an approach has a low chance of ultimate success and is only adopted by the most desperate insurgents. Iraq fit this description. Although it is unlikely that they studied Lenin, the Iraqi insurgents clearly understood the notion of "the worse, the better." Their strategy was one of mayhem designed to make the country ungovernable by the majority Shiites and other U.S. supporters.

Since Iraq teetered on the verge of chaos even without insurgent action, this was not difficult to implement. In one 12-hour stretch in August 2003, insurgents blew up the pipeline supplying water to Baghdad, fired mortar rounds into a prison holding Iraqi detainees, and set fire to a major oil pipeline.[54] Infrastructure attacks were attractive particularly because they were easier and less risky than assaults on U.S. forces. As the summer of 2003 wore on, fighting spread to new areas of Iraq beyond Baghdad and the region around

Tikrit. By August, Ramadi, west of Baghdad, saw a number of attacks on U.S. forces.[55] Violence mounted in Mosul, Iraq's third largest city and one with a mixed population.[56]

Terrorism was integral to the strategy of mayhem. In August 2003, the insurgents undertook their first truly dramatic and galvanizing terrorist attacks against civilian targets. First, a car bomb destroyed the Jordanian embassy in Baghdad, causing 19 deaths. Two weeks later, a massive car bomb exploded outside the Canal Hotel which housed the UN headquarters, killing Sergio Viera de Mello, the Secretary-General's Special Representative, and 19 others. These attacks — which may have been the work of former members of Hussein's security service or of foreign jihadists — were intended to illustrate the inability of the United States to assure security, and to deter international organizations and other nations contemplating involvement in Iraq. The insurgents and their outside supporters probably assumed that American will could be shattered by terrorism — the "Black Hawk down" syndrome. This proved wrong. Ironically, Iraqis struggled as much to understand Americans as Americans did to understand Iraqis. But the attacks also illustrated the logic of terrorism: it takes ever larger or more deadly attacks to generate a constant amount of fear. Otherwise, the victims make psychological adjustments and move on with their lives. What works yesterday may not work tomorrow. Even effective methods have a natural life span.

During the first year of the insurgency, many groups, most small and localized, competed for exposure, recognition, recruits, and financial support. Their attacks tended to be uncoordinated, but they did begin developing effective psychological methods such as producing and distributing videos or DVDs of their operations (a technique pioneered by Chechen insurgents). Because of Hussein's control of all means of communication and information, few of the insurgents initially understood the power of the Internet and the global reach of the media, but they learned quickly, building an increasingly sophisticated web presence and using Arab media such as al Jazeera to extract maximum psychological effect from their attacks.[57] In a process of natural selection, smaller and less effective groups were destroyed or merged with more successful, larger, and more prestigious ones. Gradually the insurgents settled on a four-part military strategy: causing steady U.S. casualties in order to sap American will, sabotage to prevent the return of normalcy, attacks on Iraqis supporting the new political order to deter further support, and occasional spectacular attacks and shows of force to retain the psychological initiative.[58]

To coalesce, insurgencies require time and space when security forces either are not aware of them or unable to quash them. The Iraq resistance gained such a respite because the planning assumptions used by DoD to prepare for the stabilization and transformation of Iraq did not hold. The Pentagon, CENTCOM, and the Office for Reconstruction and Humanitarian Affairs (ORHA)—the DoD organization designed to oversee the stabilization and reconstruction—all read the security situation incorrectly, assuming that the primary security problems after the removal of the Hussein regime would be revenge-taking against those associated with the former regime and sporadic, low-level attacks by the remnants of the old security forces.[59] ORHA was deeply concerned about a humanitarian crisis, given the reliance of most Iraqis on food rations from the regime, and the dislocation likely to result from the war. As Ambassador L. Paul Bremer, who later headed the U.S. occupation effort, put it, "we planned for the wrong contingency."[60] DoD and CENTCOM believed the Iraqi military and police, stripped of their top leaders, would bear primary responsibility for reestablishing order. Planners assumed that most of the security force units would remain intact and be available for duty soon after the end of conventional operations.[61] As then-National Security Adviser Rice said, "The concept was that we would defeat the army, but the institutions would hold, everything from ministries to police forces."[62] Operation Plan ECLIPSE II, the stability plan developed by the Coalition Forces Land Component Commander (CFLCC), counted on the "utilization of existing Iraqi organizations and administration."[63] Given this, CENTCOM and ORHA did not receive definitive policy guidance on the role the U.S. military was to play in public security after Hussein was removed.[64]

The Pentagon also believed that once Hussein was removed from power, other nations would contribute to the stabilization and reconstruction process. This led the Joint Staff to prepare a plan based on the presence of three multinational divisions, one a Muslim force led by the Saudis and other Gulf Arab states.[65] The multinational force was to include national police or gendarmerie to bridge the gap between conventional military units focused on combat and local police. The United States did not have organizations of this type even though they historically play a major role in stabilizing states in the aftermath of conflict. DoD assumed that power could be handed to a transitional government built on opposition leaders outside Iraq, particularly Ahmed Chalabi and other leaders of the umbrella organization known as the Iraqi National Congress. Retired Army Lieutenant General Jay Garner, the leader of ORHA, assumed that an interim Iraqi government would be functioning and ORHA withdrawn within a few months.[66] General Tommy Franks, the CENTCOM commander, instructed his subordinate commanders to expect an Iraqi government to be in place within 30 to 60 days, thus relieving them of administration and governance tasks.[67]

These planning assumptions reflected the wider changes in military strategy which the Bush administration had undertaken. "I'm committed to building a future force," President Bush stated soon after taking office, "that is defined less by size and more by mobility and swiftness, one that is easier to deploy and sustain, one that relies more heavily on stealth, precision weaponry and information technologies."[68] The Bush administration sought, as Max Boot phrased it, fully to "harness the technological advances of the information age to gain a qualitative advantage over any potential foe."[69] Secretary Rumsfeld had expended great effort to make the U.S. military faster (in both strategic and operational terms), better able to generate more combat power with fewer troops, and capable of seamless joint operations.[70] These things, he believed, would lead to a military able to do more with fewer troops. "Today," Rumsfeld stated, "speed and agility and precision can take the place of mass . . ."[71] The problem was that the new strategy of eradicating the root causes of aggression required a different skill set. Rapid conventional operations were sometimes part of such a strategy, but did not, in themselves, bring strategic success. "The insurgencies in Iraq and Afghanistan," as Lieutenant General David Petraeus puts it, "were not, in truth, the wars for which we were best prepared in 2001 . . ."[72] Or, as Brigadier Nigel Aylwin-Foster of the British Army bluntly wrote after his own service in Iraq, "the U.S. Army has developed over time a singular focus on conventional warfare, of a particularly swift and violent style, which left it ill-suited to the kind of operation it encountered as soon as conventional warfare ceased to be the primary focus. . . ."[73]

There was no easy fix for this. Other elements of the U.S. Government were not able to fill the gap. And the de facto strategic division of labor of the Clinton administration, which relied on multinational forces to shoulder the burden for long-term stabilization and reconstruction, no longer held. The decision to overthrow Saddam Hussein by force did not have the backing of the UN or of many of the nations which could have been major contributors to the stabilization and reconstruction operations. When the notion that Iraqis themselves could shoulder the burden for stabilization and reconstruction did not pan out, the United States was forced to rely on its military for precisely the type of activity that candidate Bush had criticized.

But the U.S. military was unprepared for counter-insurgency, the most complex and difficult form of stabilization. Its doctrine was decades old and designed around Cold War-style rural "people's war." Existing doctrine viewed counterinsurgency as support to a threatened but functioning regime—a situation very different from Iraq in 2003. Yet the post-Cold War model of stabilization, which assumed a relatively benign environment and a strategic division of labor, was inapplicable. The long evolution of American strategy had brought the U.S. military to the point where it faced a type of struggle that was similar to past ones, but also different in some important ways.

Doctrine and history offered only clues. There was no solution other than to learn on the fly.

**Residual Pockets of Resistance.**

During the crucial weeks and months after the removal of the Hussein regime, the U.S. military and other elements of the government were not prepared for the magnitude of the task they faced. As Isaiah Wilson notes, CENTCOM never developed a truly comprehensive plan for Phase IV of the campaign — stabilizing Iraq and handing administration off to civilian authorities.[74] The military units in Iraq were exhausted from months of training and intense combat operations. They had prepared for warfighting, not occupation and stabilization.[75] According to an operations officer from a task force of the 1st Infantry Division, "While we were very well trained for conventional warfare against a conventional enemy, we did not receive appreciable training in counterinsurgency operations."[76] Or as a brigade commander from the 1st Armored Division phrased it, unit "training focused on high-intensity combat and not on the type of operations in which the brigade found itself when it arrived in Baghdad."[77] There were too few forces, leaving important parts of Iraq without a U.S. presence, particularly Iraq's western Anbar province which included the cities of Fallujah and Ramadi. As Secretary Rumsfeld admitted, these areas were largely bypassed in the war, leaving Hussein loyalists a free rein.[78] The unstated assumption seemed to be that the combat prowess of the American military would intimidate any opponents of the occupation into submission. But as earlier U.S. experience in Lebanon and Somalia showed, this did not always work when American forces intervened in a society with a warrior tradition reinforced by religious conviction. The U.S. military was configured to break the will of conventional opponents through rapid decisive operations, not to break the will of an irregular opponent through protracted psychological and political actions.

The organizations designed to lead the political and economic reconstruction of Iraq equally were ill-prepared. ORHA was under- and incorrectly staffed, and had little time to prepare for its mission.[79] Some personnel were selected for political credentials rather than expertise.[80] The relationship between the military and ORHA was problematic from the beginning.[81] Phase IV planners at CFLCC did not coordinate with ORHA.[82] One staff member wrote in a memo that "ORHA is not treated seriously enough by the command (CENTCOM)."[83] Military officers complained that ORHA and the Coalitional Provisional Authority (CPA—the renamed and redesigned occupation authority under Ambassador Bremer) were ineffective or absent all together.[84] A brigade commander from the 101st Airborne Division (Air Assault) noted "philosophical differences on everything from local governance to the selection and training of local security forces" between the military and ORHA/CPA.[85] The military had resources and a widespread presence, but no specific mandate for reconstruction or an overarching national strategic plan to indicate how to do so. ORHA had the mandate, but not the resources. ORHA personnel could not even travel around Baghdad without support from the military, and it certainly did not have the personnel and money needed to undertake what needed to be done and done quickly. Nor did it have a detailed plan to address the conditions it found in Iraq.[86]

There also were problems deciding what to make of the violence in Iraq. When it first emerged, DoD portrayed it as a combination of criminal opportunism and the last spasms of a few lingering Hussein loyalists.[87] Secretary Rumsfeld blamed "people who were the enforcers for the Saddam Hussein regime—the Fedayeen Saddam people and the Ba'ath Party members and undoubtedly some of his security guards" and "50 to 100 thousand prison inmates who were put back out in the street, criminals of various types."[88] In early May, General Richard Myers, Chairman of the Joint Chiefs of Staff, noted, "we continue to root out residual pockets of resistance from paramilitary forces and Ba'ath Party personnel."[89] During a June press conference, Ambassador Bremer also characterized the attacks on American forces as originating from small groups of "Fedayeen Saddam or former Republican Guard officers."[90] This led American leaders to conclude that there was no need for a comprehensive counterinsurgency strategy, but only for continued vigilance and assertive action until the criminals and the former regime loyalists grew tired, were caught, or were killed.

CENTCOM did attempt to address the problem by sending more military police and shifting infantry to police duties.[91] Some combat units tackled the infrastructure problems which were generating public anger, often on their own volition.[92] Such steps were only partially successful. Many units felt that they had accomplished what they were sent to do—remove Hussein's regime—and assumed a passive stance waiting to be relieved.[93] Some officers on the ground warned that using combat troops for civic action or pacification was ineffective since they were not trained, organized, or equipped for it. And even units that did attempt to restore local order and stoke reconstruction found it a double-edged sword: they then were blamed by the Iraqi public when things went awry or when street violence and infrastructure problems interfered with daily life.[94]

Almost immediately, questions arose about the adequacy of the U.S. troop presence. This was the beginning of a long debate which reflected one of the psychological dilemmas of counterinsurgency, particularly when it is undertaken by an outside force. Having more American forces would have deterred some insurgent operations and might have made some Iraqis feel more secure, but it also would have antagonized many other Iraqis, given their distaste for outside occupation, particularly by non-Muslims. It was truly a "damned if we do, damned if we don't" decision. But senior policymakers, once they recognized that they could not count on Iraqis themselves to secure the country, extended the tour of units already in-country.[95] Responding to charges that they had become too passive, U.S. military commanders more than doubled the number of patrols in Baghdad, seeking a continuous presence in key neighborhoods.[96] More American units were also moved to the restive Sunni Arab areas west of Baghdad.[97]

The northern region around Mosul and the southern Shiite regions around Basra, Karbala, and Najaf were far from placid but at least somewhat more stable. According to Lieutenant General David McKiernan, then serving as the Coalition's Joint Task Force (CJTF) Seven Commander, Iraq's south was considered "permissive," the north "semi-permissive," but the central area included some "hot spots."[98] In Mosul, the 101st Airborne Division under the command of Major General David Petraeus moved quickly into the political vacuum and worked vigorously to restore economic activity and generate a functioning Iraqi administration.[99] The division undertook the "non-standard" tasks associated with stabilization and reconstruction, reestablishing Iraqi administration of the area, developing support and liaison relationships with all elements of local governance and administration, helping Iraqis begin a reconciliation commission to deal with those associated with the Hussein regime, building an intelligence Joint Interagency Task Force using the expertise of Bosnia veterans, and adopting the Multiyear Road Map approach to planning which also had been successful in Bosnia. In the south, British units, long accustomed to a less confrontational method of occupation in Northern Ireland and occupying a Shiite area, also faced fewer problems.[100]

Since CENTCOM and the Pentagon identified Hussein supporters as the main cause of the violence, CJTF 7 became more aggressive, approaching stabilization as a variant of warfighting. Displaying what General John Abizaid called the "offensive spirit in a tough place," U.S. forces went on the attack, staging a series of raids and sweeps across the Sunni triangle.[101] While these operations killed or captured a number of resistance fighters, they also antagonized the public in those regions and probably inspired many to join the insurgency. Edward Luttwak has pointed out that strategy in general operates with a "paradoxical logic" — what appears to be the best or most effective action often is not since strategy pits two (or more) scheming opponents, each attempting to thwart the other.[102] The paradoxical logic is at its most intense in counterinsurgency with its multilayered psychological complexity and multiple audiences and participants. What appears to be the best or most effective action in tangible terms often has unintended and deleterious effects in the psychological domain. Counterinsurgents must simultaneously kill or capture active insurgents while they degrade public support for the insurgency or passivity. But actions which do one of these things often degrade the other. The most effective methods for eliminating insurgents can alienate or anger the public.

David Galula, a French army officer, noted that counterinsurgency often involves a "vicious cycle" when military operations turn the public against the military and the military, in turn then begins to see the public as the enemy, thus amplifying the mutual hostility and making it more difficult to win public acceptance or support.[103] The June and July offensives suggested that the vicious cycle had begun. They probably angered more Iraqis than they captured, leading to an aggregate increase in support for the resistance and convincing many that the United States was an occupier, not a liberator.[104] When civilians were killed or mistreated during raids, it increased sympathy and outright support for the resistance.[105] Methods used by American forces during arrests of suspected insurgents were particularly antagonizing. After interviewing a number of detainees, the International Committee of the Red Cross (ICRC) wrote:

> Arresting authorities entered houses usually after dark, breaking down doors, waking up residents roughly, yelling orders, forcing family members into tins room (sic) under military guard while searching the rest of the house and further breaking doors, cabinets and other property. They arrested suspects, tying their hands in the back with flexi-cuffs, hooding them, and taking them away. Sometimes they arrested all adult males present in a house, including elderly, handicapped or sick people. Treatment often included pushing people around, insulting, taking aim with rifles, punching and kicking

and striking with rifles. Individuals were often led away in whatever they happened to be wearing at the time of arrest—sometimes in pyjamas or underwear - and were denied the opportunity to gather a few essential belongings, such as clothing, hygiene items, medicine or eyeglasses. Those who surrendered with a suitcase often had their belongings confiscated. In many cases personal belongings were seized during the arrest, with no receipt being issued. Certain CF (Coalition Forces) military intelligence officers told the ICRC that in their estimate between 70% and 90% of the persons deprived of their liberty in Iraq had been arrested by mistake.[106]

Whether accurate or not, this was the perception among the Iraqi population. And in counterinsurgency, perception matters more than reality. Even though most of those arrested by mistake were quickly released, they considered themselves dishonored, often in front of their families, thus amplifying anger, resentment, and hostility. At least some American units treated everyone as potential insurgents. This became a self-fulfilling prophecy. Some U.S. commanders grasped this, others did not. The hostility of the Iraqi public then hardened. This angered the American troops, particularly those who had lost friends in combat. By the end of his unit's tour, for instance, a company commander in the 4th Infantry Division advised officers coming after him to remember, "most of the people here want us dead, they hate us and everything we stand for, and will take any opportunity to cause us harm."[107] In the broadest sense, Americans had forgotten, after 225 years of independence, the humiliation and anger that comes from foreign occupation. They had as much difficulty understanding why Iraqis resisted efforts to help and protect them as British colonialists had in the 1770s.

In the early months of the insurgency, American commanders struggled to find the most effective balance between the "mailed fist" and the "velvet glove." They adjusted tactics to place greater emphasis on intelligence gathering, winning public support, "friendly persuasion," and limited civilian casualties and destruction.[108] The Commander's Emergency Response Program (CERP), which CPA created with captured Iraqi money, allowed military commanders to undertake small projects with limited red tape.[109] Senior military leaders considered this program "highly important" and felt that had even more funds been available, it could have made a difference during the vital first months of occupation.[110] Some complained that new restrictions on CERP implemented in the autumn seriously hurt stabilization efforts. But despite all of this, the "velvet glove" approach never fully overcame the perception among significant sections of the Iraq public that the occupation itself was the source of their frustration and anger.[111] Ultimately counterinsurgency is determined less by which side the public prefers to rule it than by which side they blame for their suffering. By the summer of 2003, it was clear that at least in the Sunni Arab community, the United States was held responsible. And, at the same time, an increasing influx of foreign jihadists further fueled the fire, transforming it, to some Iraqis, into a spiritual struggle rather than simply a political conflict.

**A Massive and Long-Term Undertaking.**

As soon as Ambassador Bremer arrived in Iraq, he recognized that the initial idea of constructing an Iraq government quickly and handing over power to it would not work. The country needed an extended period of U.S. tutelage to adjust to the complexities of open governance.[112] As President Bush noted, the United States faced a "massive and long-term undertaking" there.[113] This forced the military to adjust its thinking. With the new strategic time frame and growing instability, administration policymakers realized that the U.S. military would need a significant number of troops in Iraq for an extended period of time. This required long-term rotation plans, addressing the problem of "high demand, low density" units such as military police and intelligence specialists, and building adequate military infrastructure.[114] The rotation issue was particularly thorny. Neither the Army nor the Marine Corps were configured for large scale, protracted stabilization operations, but for either relatively short, intense wars or modest involvement in protracted peacekeeping. By September, the Army and Marine Corps were feeling the stress both in terms of troop rotations and budgets.[115] The Congressional Budget Office published a widely-discussed report that questioned the ability of the Army to sustain its rotation in Iraq beyond March 2004 without extending tours beyond 1 year or other radical actions.[116] Service leaders were becoming increasingly concerned about the effect that combat tours in Iraq would have on recruitment and retention, and thus on their ability to field a force of the desired quality.[117]

The Pentagon pursued several solutions. In the most immediate sense, it sought to squeeze as much as possible from available resources. The Army activated additional National Guard and Reserve forces for service in Iraq.[118] Nearly every active duty unit in the Army was added to the planned troop rotation, tours were extended for both active and reserve units, and training and education cycles were adjusted to maximize the troops available for deployment.[119] In Iraq, commanders accepted the fact that they could only provide a limited presence in parts of the country. At the policy level, the administration actively sought partners who would send troops. While the coalition eventually included several dozen participants, most of them provided only small contingents.[120] A few nations like India and Turkey considered larger deployments, but decided against it.[121] This was frustrating. Administration officials seem to have believed that even states which opposed the use of force to overthrow Saddam Hussein would recognize the high stakes involved and pitch in. In reality, many nations were willing to let Iraq teeter on chaos rather than legitimize and support American policy. The problem, as Francis Fukuyama notes, was that "The Bush administration and its neoconservative supporters failed to anticipate the hostility of the global reaction to the [Iraq] war before undertaking it, particularly in Europe."[122] The same held for other Arab states and members of the 1991 Operation DESERT STORM coalition. Many had decided that instability in Iraq was less of a threat than unchecked American power.

Once U.S. policymakers and military leaders recognized that they faced a growing insurgency rather than a mopping up operation, they knew that the ultimate solution was a new Iraqi military and security force.[123] But Ambassador Bremer's decisions to disband the old army and prohibit Iraqis who had held positions in the old regime from participating in the new security services complicated this. In June 2003 CPA announced plans to create a new military from scratch. It hoped for an initial force of 12,000 within a year, with an ultimate goal of 40,000—a size deemed large enough for national defense but not so large as to intimidate neighboring states or provide Baghdad with a tool for renewed aggression.[124] CPA also created a separate civil defense force to guard key installations and infrastructure.[125] In October 2003, U.S. officials announced a four-phase plan designed to turn responsibility over to Iraqi security forces as soon as they were ready.[126] A few weeks later, CPA increased the pace of Iraqi force development.[127] Despite this, everyone recognized this would be a slow process (since it takes about 2 years to form a division).[128]

DoD also instigated long-term programs to improve the U.S. military's capabilities for counterinsurgency and similar operations. Most important were "rebalancing" and "modularizing" the Army. Rebalancing was a program to assure that soldiers were placed where their skills were needed. It also involved "civilianizing" a number of jobs to free soldiers for other duties. Modularization was a new way to package forces, tailoring units to missions.[129] By shifting from a division-based to a brigade-based structure, the Army expected to increase the combat power of the active component by 30 percent and augment flexibility without an overall increase in force size.[130] This was combined with the Army Force Generation Model (ARFORGEN), a new tool to coordinate readiness and training cycles.[131]

All of this was useful, but critics contended that even a modularized Army at its existing size could not undertake protracted stabilization operations, continue transformation, perform its other worldwide missions, and sustain the quality of its troops, leaders, and equipment. The only solution, they felt, was increasing the overall size of the American military, particularly the ground forces.[132] Bipartisan support formed in Congress for enlarging the Army.[133] Secretary Rumsfeld, however, resisted the idea, arguing that increasing the size of the Army would drain resources from defense transformation.[134] "The real problem," he wrote, "is not necessarily the size of our active and reserve military components, per se, but rather how forces have been managed, and the mix of capabilities at our disposal."[135] Iraq was at the center of the debate over the size of the Army. Secretary Rumsfeld and General Abizaid contended that increasing troop strength would simply put U.S. forces at greater risk and sidetrack the development of the Iraqi security forces.[136] This reflected a lesson the Bush administration had drawn from U.S. involvement in the Balkans: other nations have less incentive to assume responsibility for the security of their nation or region if the United States does it for them. If the United States limits its role, others will increase theirs. It was strategic "tough love." Unfortunately, it did not pan out in Iraq, leading defense analysts, members of Congress, and CPA administrator Bremer to argue that the only solution was more American troops.[137]

**They Had the Training to Stand and Fight.**

Even as the United States adjusted its counter-insurgency campaign, the insurgency itself evolved. One of the most ominous trends was the influx of foreign jihadists, some affiliated with al-Qai'da. While the jihadists only composed a small proportion of the resistance, their willingness to undertake suicide attacks escalated the danger to American forces and the sense of fear among Iraqis. It also raised the strategic stakes of the conflict, making it more clearly part of the war on terror.[138] In response, Lieutenant General Ricardo Sanchez, commander of the U.S. forces, was forced to devote more attention to finding and eradicating foreign fighters.[139] This meant less time and fewer resources for other activities, including reconstruction.

The resistance continued to show improved tactical ability.[140] By the autumn of 2003, there were 35 attacks a day across Iraq. The insurgents seemed to understand that they could create the maximum fear (and publicity) by combining low level violence which made daily life dangerous with occasional large, high-profile attacks. Humans can tolerate much danger if it is in constant and expected doses. The anticipation of a different kind or level of danger, though, increases anxiety which, in turn, saps morale and will. Following this logic, the insurgents launched a rocket attack on the Rashid Hotel in Baghdad during a visit by Deputy Secretary of Defense Paul Wolfowitz in October.[141] This killed an American lieutenant colonel—the highest ranking officer to die in the conflict to that point. More importantly, it demonstrated to the Americans that no place in Iraq was safe. As always in insurgency, the military effect of an operation was much less important than the psychological one. During the same time, insurgents struck three Baghdad police stations and the headquarters of the International Committee of the Red Cross simultaneously.[142] This also served multiple psychological purposes, illustrating that the insurgents could coordinate complex operations and deterring the type of relief and reconstruction efforts which might be able to blunt public frustration. The worse, the better.

During October 2003, insurgent attacks surged in what American officials called the "Ramadan offensive." In November, insurgents downed a U.S. Army CH-47 transport helicopter, killing 15. At the time, this was the single worst attack on U.S. forces since the end of major combat operations. The insurgents stepped up assaults on less committed coalition members including Spain, Japan, and South Korea.[143] The fighting spread to regions that had been stable, particularly Mosul.[144]

By December, a third of the first battalion of the new Iraqi army, which had been sworn in during October, had deserted.[145] While it eventually died out, the Ramadan offensive showed new levels of coordination and resolve by the insurgents.[146] After a pitched battle in Samarra, a U.S. Army officer said, "Here it seems they had the training to stand and fight."[147]

Like Tet 1968 in Vietnam or the January 1981 national offensive of the *Frente Farabundo Marti de Liberación Nacional* (FMLN) in El Salvador, the Ramadan offensive tried to demonstrate the insurgency's courage and power, expose the weakness of the Coalition and, galvanize public support.[148] As in those earlier offensives, the insurgents suffered a tactical defeat but made psychological gains. U.S. Government assessments soon after the offensive provided a bleak picture, noting that a growing number of Iraqis believed the insurgents could defeat the United States.[149] Eventually November 2003 ended as the deadliest month for the United States to that point, surpassing the conventional battles of March and April. In response, military units heightened the emphasis they gave to force protection. Again, the paradoxical logic was at play: limiting casualties was good for morale and public support but hindered pacification. In November, Clay McManaway, a retired ambassador serving as CPA deputy, gave Bremer a paper, arguing that the Army had gone into a "passive mode." Operations were not running at the same tempo as over the summer, and some units had cut back on patrolling.[150]

While ebbs and flows are normal in counter-insurgency, the Bush administration could not take the continued support of the American public and the Congress for granted. Counterinsurgency seldom involves constant, demonstrable progress and quick

37

resolution, but that was what the American public had come to expect of military operations after Operation DESERT STORM. In the decades after Vietnam, the public and Congress appeared to have forgotten what insurgency was like. The administration thus realized that it only had a limited period of time before public and congressional support eroded. The dilemma was whether to seek the quickest possible transfer of responsibility to Iraqi security forces, or a modulated pace of change that did not demand more of the new Iraqi forces than they could provide, thus maximizing the chances that Iraq would end up stable and democratic.[151] Strategic failure, in other words, could come from two sources: the collapse of the new Iraqi government and security forces, or the collapse of American will. The Bush administration had to navigate a treacherous course between these dangers.

The capture of Saddam Hussein in December 2003 briefly gave American forces the psychological initiative. Hopes were that it would convince the Iraqi public that the future did, in fact, lie with the new government.[152] U.S. military leaders, though, recognized that Hussein's role in the insurgency mostly was symbolic, so his capture would not break it.[153] Attacks on U.S. forces declined for a while, but picked up again early in 2004, with an increase in the use of sophisticated roadside bombs.[154] Assaults on Iraqis associated with the Americans, particularly serving and candidate police officers, were relentless, with more than 400 killed by March 2004.[155] With some former regime officials demoralized by Hussein's capture, the role of foreign jihadists correspondingly increased. They began creating cells which included native Iraqis.[156] Once again, Fallujah was at the fore. Outside fighters, many linked to al-Qai'da in some way, began streaming into the city, forming working partnerships or loose alliances with locals.[157] "The Fallujah region is filling up with Wahabis," said a tribal leader.[158] By February 2004, it was difficult to know who actually was in charge of the city — the U.S.-sanctioned local government or the insurgents.[159]

This came at a treacherous time for the U.S. military, with 110,000 new troops scheduled to replace 130,000 who had finished their 12-month tour early in the year.[160] The massive rotation involved eight of the Army's ten active divisions, a Marine Expeditionary Force (MEF), and 40,000 international troops. It was the largest since World War II. This raised several concerns. One was that some of the local knowledge and expertise gained by the outgoing troops, which is an invaluable commodity in stabilization and counterinsurgency, would be lost. In addition, the total number of U.S. forces would go down after the rotation.[161] The insurgents, DoD feared, would recognize this and escalate attacks on U.S. forces.[162] And since there was a greater proportion of reservists in the incoming forces, this would further stress the services, causing additional problems with recruitment and retention in both the Active and Reserve components.[163]

While there was some temporary loss of capability during the rotation, it went fairly well. Certainly it was not the disaster that it could have been, in large part because of astute management by CENTCOM's commanders. The incoming units were better trained, organized, and equipped for stabilization and counterinsurgency than those they replaced, thus allowing them to adjust more quickly.[164] Units scheduled for direct replacement — for instance, the 1st Cavalry Division and the 1st Armored Division, and the 101st Airborne and Task Force Olympia — established contact several months in advance of the rotation to share lessons and information in three vital areas: 1) counterinsurgency procedures; 2) specific information about the area of operations, especially concerning the insurgent units there; and, 3) how to get things done in the complex national administrative system involving CPA and the Iraqi Governing Council. Incoming units undertook "leaders' reconnaissance" before deploying and sent staff members in advance of the units' deployment. Outgoing units left key staff members behind to help with continuity. A key step was what became known as "left seat/right seat rides" during the overlap, with incoming commanders participating in operations with the units they were to replace.[165]

In addition, a web of informal communications for information between junior leaders and noncommissioned officers had emerged, relying on email and Internet sites.[166] While this caused some concern among senior leaders, it did facilitate the hand-off. The pressure of counterinsurgency operations was, in Dr. Leonard Wong's words, creating a cohort of junior officers "learning to be adaptable, creative, innovative, and confident in their abilities to handle just about any task thrown at them."[167] Information technology provided the means to pass this along.

In general, the first year of the counterinsurgency was a time of rapid learning for the U.S. military. It had made great strides in many areas. Still, U.S. strategy had shortcomings. This particularly was evident toward the end of 2003 as mounting casualties and hostility from the Iraqi public, combined with the inherent aggressiveness of the military's warfighting ethos, led some American units to concentrate more on eliminating insurgents than dominating the psychological battlespace. As Major General George

Fay later noted in his investigation of the Abu Ghraib Detention Facility, "as the pace of operations picked up in late November–early December 2003, it became a common practice for maneuver elements to round up large quantities of Iraqi personnel in the general vicinity of a specified target as a cordon and capture technique."[168] Such actions did eliminate enemy fighters, but they also amplified public anger and resentment. In many cases, operations which were successful militarily were political and psychological losses, inspiring new recruits or supporters for the insurgency. While most U.S. commanders understood the psychological priorities of counterinsurgency and acted accordingly, they were overshadowed by the negative effects of those who did not. To concentrate on eliminating enemy fighters rather than discrediting them or undercutting their support was very much within the U.S. military's tradition—it was a strategy of attrition in which victory came from killing or capturing enemy combatants until the opponent's will collapsed. This often worked in conventional war. It had, after all, led the United States to stunning victories in World War II and the Gulf War. But, history suggests, it seldom brings success in counterinsurgency.

## A Powerful, Deeply Symbolic Myth.

By the spring of 2004, the growing influence of outside jihadists within the insurgency pushed it toward more extreme positions and a greater focus on terrorism.[169] Insurgent leaders had begun to believe that the Americans would soon be gone, leaving them to the second and decisive part of their struggle—war against the Shiites. A letter written by Abu Musab al-Zarqawi, the brutal Jordanian-born leader of al-Qai'da in Iraq, offered a stark illustration. He, at least, sought outright sectarian war between Shiites and Sunnis. The letter said:

> . . . Shiism is the looming danger and the true challenge. They are the enemy. Beware of them. Fight them. By God, they lie...Most of the Sunnis are aware of the danger of these people, watch their sides, and fear the consequences of empowering them.[170]

The jihadists quickly put this concept into practice, using suicide bombers to attack participants at the religious festival of Ashura in Karbala and Baghdad, killing 140.[171] While Iraq's Shiites recognized the threat to their community from the Sunni Arabs, this did not translate into full support for the occupation and American-engineered transition. Many of them grudgingly accepted the U.S. presence, but others appeared to believe that, with Iranian support, they could take care of themselves.

At the same time, the American forces continued refining their tactical and operational methods. After less than a year, the insurgency had taken a classic form: a deadly learning contest between insurgents and counterinsurgents. Much of the adaptation involved tactics, techniques, and procedures, especially ones designed to deal with roadside bombs.[172] Within days of some innovation by the insurgents, countermeasures were in place and integrated into the training of units preparing for deployment.[173] U.S. forces placed more emphasis on encouraging Iraqi security forces to lead operations.[174] Newly deploying units used what then-Major General Peter W. Chiarelli, commander of the 1st Cavalry Division, called "full spectrum operations" which tightly integrated combat with training and reconstruction efforts.[175]

Despite this, the insurgents also improved and expanded. Rather than "shoot and scoot" attacks, they undertook set-piece small unit actions—what one U.S. officer described as "a stand-up fight between two military forces."[176] They attempted to create and hold "liberated areas."[177] In April 2004, violence spread to new parts of Iraq, including previously quiet parts of Baghdad and the northern city of Kirkuk.[178] In the south, Shiite militias under the control of Moqtada Sadr launched an offensive against the coalition.[179] Eventually major battles took place in half a dozen cities.[180] Fighting in Fallujah reached a new peak as the Coalition decided to clear the city after a well-publicized and particularly brutal attack on American security contractors.[181] During the battle, Sunni Arab insurgents and Shiite militias openly cooperated for the first time.[182] Facing bitterly hostile coverage from the Arab media and intense pressure from the Iraqi Governing Council and influential clerics like Grand Ayatollah Sistani, American officials feared a united Sunni-Shiite resistance, a nation-wide popular uprising, and derailment of the political transition.[183] Washington called off the assault on Fallujah with parts of the city still under insurgent control. Responsibility for security was given to a cobbled-together Iraqi unit called the "Fallujah Brigade" which quickly proved worthless.[184] Most of the hard-core militants simply faded away to fight another day.[185] By June 2004, the Shiite uprising in Iraq's south had abated, but insurgents ruled the streets of Fallujah and implemented a Taliban-like, austere form of Islamic law.[186] Foreign fighters controlled whole neighborhoods.[187] Fallujah served as a major guerrilla base where insurgents could plan and launch attacks across the Sunni triangle.[188]

The insurgents portrayed the battle as a stunning victory. As Anthony Cordesman noted, it "created the image of large innocent casualties, a 'heroic' Iraqi opposition, collateral damage, and U.S. advanced weapons hitting mosques."[189] Other observers talked of a "powerful, deeply symbolic myth" emerging from Fallujah.[190] This was an important idea: myth creation is often the goal of major insurgent offensives. Insurgency, after all, is armed theater. In past insurgencies, events such as the Battle of Algiers, Dien Bien Phu, and the Tet Offensive had symbolic impact far beyond their military effect. What became known as "first Fallujah" played a similar role. Myth was particularly important in Iraq. Hussein's tight control of information had left the Iraqi public poorly prepared to distinguish truth from disinformation, thus amplifying the effects of insurgent propaganda.[191] It was the paradoxical logic at play again: crushing battlefield defeats do not deal decisive psychological blows to insurgents, but battlefield defeats which can be portrayed as "glorious" become psychological victories for them.

Ultimately, Fallujah did not have the impact of Tet or Dien Bien Phu but did increase sympathy for the insurgents, both within Iraq and elsewhere in the Islamic world.[192] It also had a polarizing effect, eroding the number of neutrals among the Iraqi public and driving the majority into one camp or the other.[193] Even in the United States, the furor of the April 2004 battles increased criticism of the counterinsurgency strategy and was the beginning of a long decline in public and congressional support for American involvement.[194] As always, trends and expectations were central in the evolution of the insurgency. Politically and psychologically at least, Fallujah was an insurgent victory, creating a sense among the insurgents and their supporters that victory was possible, and raising the idea within the United States that defeat could happen.[195]

By demonstrating how far the Iraqis had to go before they could defend themselves without extensive American help, the April battles renewed concern for the effect the conflict was having on the U.S. military. General Abizaid announced that he needed more troops than he had planned for, but indicated that he would draw them from elsewhere in the CENTCOM area rather than asking DoD for additional ones.[196] The Army again extended the tours of some units in Iraq, returned others to the country more quickly than planned, and began exploring policies such as shorter leaves.[197] While the Army met its reenlistment goals through the spring of 2004, with the next rotation into Iraq including an even higher proportion of reservists, service leaders remained concerned.[198] Reports that the Army was experiencing a significant dip in readiness renewed calls for increasing its size.[199] Key modernization plans, particularly the development and fielding of the future combat system (FCS) were delayed in part due to the operational costs of Iraq.[200] General Peter Schoomaker, the Army Chief of Staff, admitted that Iraq was "stressing" the Army but advised that he could support at least 3 more years of involvement in Iraq at existing levels without a force increase.[201] Trouble, though, lay ahead. "What keeps me awake at night," General Richard Cody, Army Vice Chief of Staff, told Congress, "is what will this all-volunteer force look like in 2007."[202]

The April battles also showed the mixed quality of the Iraqi security forces. While those trained by the British in the south or the 101st Airborne in the north did well, many others simply melted away. According to General Abizaid, "a number of units, both in the police force and also in the ICDC [Iraqi Civil Defense Corps], did not stand up to the intimidators of the forces of

Sadr's militia and that was a great disappointment to us."[203] The Pentagon quickly dispatched Major General Petraeus back to Baghdad to energize the training program.[204]

Sadr's uprising illustrated the growing problem of sectarian militias. The country was full of them. Most important were the Kurdish peshmergas, a force of 70,000 which had emerged in the 1990s to protect the autonomous regions in Iraq's north from Hussein's forces; the Badr Corps of the Supreme Council for Islamic Revolution in Iraq (SCIRI), a Shiite movement with strong ties to Iran; and Sadr's "Mahdi Army."[205] Ambassador Bremer wanted the militias dissolved, and assigned veteran diplomat David Gompert to lead the effort. The leaders of the militias, of course, opposed this idea, recognizing that their armed groups were central to their authority, serving as a check on both rival factions and the new government. As the date for the handover of sovereignty from CPA to the Iraqi government approached, little progress had been made.

The militia issue showed one of the shortcomings in the way that the United States, armed with a concept of insurgency forged while fighting communist forces during the Cold War, thought about the Iraq conflict. In Cold War counterinsurgency, the most important actors were the antagonists themselves—the regime and the insurgents—and, in most cases, state sponsors of one side or the other. But one of the important, even defining, features of 21st century insurgency was the growing role of what might be called "third" and "fourth" forces. Third forces were armed organizations sometimes affiliated with either the insurgents or the regime, sometimes autonomous. They included militias, criminal gangs, warlord armies, and various kinds of death squads, all influencing the conduct and outcome of the insurgency. While these had participated or affected insurgencies for a number of years—Colombia is the best example—Iraq added a new and very important third force to the mix: security contractors who performed many of the functions that state counterinsurgent forces could not or would not. This raised new questions of morality, legality, and efficacy. It also added new layers of complexity to the paradoxical logic of counterinsurgency. Many security contractors, for instance, guarded coalition officials. Their mission was to protect their client by any means necessary. In many cases, the way they did this ran counter to the larger strategic objective of winning Iraqi support.[206]

Fourth forces in insurgency were unarmed nonstate organizations which affected the conduct and outcome of the conflict. They include international organizations, nongovernmental organizations involved in relief and reconstruction, private voluntary organizations, the international media, and international finance and business (which influence the conflict by deciding to invest or not invest in the country). Both third and fourth forces played a central role in Iraq: al Jazeera and other Arab and Iranian broadcasting organizations played a major role in shaping public opinion in Iraq, in the region, and in other parts of the world. But neither the U.S. military nor CPA had effective programs to deal with them. Doctrine offered little guidance on how to do so.

With the return of sovereignty to the Iraqi government approaching in June 2004, the U.S. military continued its shift from a leading to a supporting role. As Colonel Dana Pittard of the 1st Infantry Division phrased it, the Americans moved from a role of "partnership and occupation" to one of "partnership and support."[207] U.S. units became involved more heavily in protecting Iraqi officials and infrastructure, gradually giving Iraqi security forces the lead on counterinsurgency strikes and sweeps.[208] General George Casey, who had replaced General Sanchez as overall commander of coalition military forces, focused on synchronization of the "mailed fist" and the "velvet glove." He established a Counterinsurgency Academy to assure that incoming unit commanders understood this.[209] The United States created the Multinational Security Training Command — Iraq (MNSTC-I) to coordinate security force development with the new Iraqi government.[210] As the CPA, which was a DoD organization, prepared to dissolve, the State Department was establishing one of the largest American embassies in the world in Baghdad.[211]

While the diminution of the U.S. role in the insurgency was a good thing—history suggested that the United States was most successful at counterinsurgency when it supported local partners rather than dominating the effort—the timing was problematic. The new Iraqi security forces simply were not ready to replace U.S. units on a one-for-one basis. It as not so much a matter of raw numbers as of combat effectiveness. Few Iraqi units could undertake autonomous actions or even a leading role. Nor did they have the vital support they needed in terms of logistics, intelligence, and other functions. Scaling back U.S.-led combat operations left the insurgents virtually free of pressure in parts of Iraq, particularly the far western Anbar province.[212] As with the militias, a major issue was thus postponed rather than addressed as all efforts focused on the handover to the Iraqis.

American officials feared that the insurgents would launch another offensive during the June 2004 political transition. There was, in fact, an upsurge in violence. The week before the planned transfer on June 30, intense fighting raged in Fallujah, Ramadi, Baqubah, Mosul, and Baghdad.[213] To an extent, though, the offensive was weaker than expected. In part, this reflected a schism within the insurgency. Some Sunni Arab nationalists sympathetic to the resistance were concerned that foreign jihadists like Zarqawi had hijacked the movement and driven it toward objectives of little concern to most Iraqis or even antithetical to their wishes.[214] Clearly there was still tension within the Sunni Arab community between the sectarian view of the conflict pushed by Zarqawi and the more nationalist perspective which held that Iraqi Shiites — at least those not overtly affiliated with Iran — still were Iraqis. Feelings about the political transition itself were mixed within the Sunni Arab community. Some favored allowing it, apparently because it would speed the withdrawal of the Americans. Others seemed to believe that interfering with the political transition (and sustaining the American presence) would work to their benefit by stoking public anger. As time wore on, most of the insurgents fell into the latter camp, taking a hands-off approach to national elections.

The attacks on civilians during preparations for the June 2004 transition of political authority illustrated one of the perennial challenges insurgents face — they also must modulate the form and extent of their violence, attempting to enflame dissatisfaction with the regime, provoke overreaction, and deter support for the government without alienating the public. Insurgents, too, must walk a fine line. The execution of hostages and suicide attacks on Shiite religious gatherings generated much publicity for the insurgents but also increased hostility. By the summer of 2004 — with the insurgency a year old — most of the resistance appeared to have abandoned the beheadings, probably because the negative reaction outweighed the benefits, but they continued other forms of terrorism.

### The Prospect of an Outright Victory.

The June 2004 transfer of political power did not stop the resistance. Insurgents continued attacking U.S. forces, Iraqis associated with the Americans or the government, and infrastructure. A massacre of 50 unarmed Iraqi National Guard recruits showed the brutal extent this could reach.[215] As the autumn of 2004 began, American officials admitted that the insurgents had near-control over important parts of central Iraq, especially the cities of Fallujah, Ramadi, Samarra, and Baqubah.[216] Experts warned that the movement could be undertaking the classic development pattern of insurgencies, first creating "liberated zones" then building a conventional capability.[217] To U.S. and Iraqi officials, this was unacceptable. Fallujah particularly was worrisome and was seen by both the insurgents and the counterinsurgents as the epicenter of the resistance. Its "myth" persisted. In November U.S. forces launched a second, larger, and much better-planned offensive to clear it, driving the insurgents out after bitter fighting.[218] Squeezed out of Fallujah, insurgents launched fierce counterattacks elsewhere, particularly in Mosul.[219] Continuing the strategy of mayhem, they executed a number of Kurdish policemen and militia members.[220]

But as parts of the insurgency undertook sectarian terrorism, tension within the movement continued as the resistance itself stumbled on the paradoxical logic of insurgency. There were reports of outright battles between Iraqis and foreign jihadists.[221] In January 2005, a group affiliated with al-Qai'da took credit for a bombing which killed Shiite cleric Sheikh Mahmoud al-Madaini, a senior aide to Grand Ayatollah Sistani.[222] A few weeks later suicide bombers again struck Shiite worshipers in and around Baghdad during important holy days, killing at least 30.[223] Eventually the Shiite community lost patience.[224] Shiite militias began engaging insurgents in gun battles and undertaking reprisals for insurgent attacks. Mysterious deaths of Sunnis were rumored to be the work of Shiite death squads, perhaps linked to the police or other elements of the security services.[225] Attacks on Shiites, the International Crisis Group found, "are countered by sweeps through predominantly Sunni towns and neighbourhoods by men dressed in police uniforms accused of belonging to the commando units of the ministry of interior."[226]

Despite this, the political process continued. To help assure security for the important January 2005 national elections, CENTCOM increased the American troop presence in Iraq from 17 to 20 brigades—its highest level.[227] This was successful. While the insurgents and radical clerics kept voter turnout light in Sunni areas, the election went smoothly in the rest of the country, striking a political and psychological blow to the resistance. The world press exploded with pictures of Iraqis jubilant over their first freely cast vote. Iraqis knew that it was mostly their own security forces which kept order during the election. Public sentiment appeared to shift away from the insurgents.[228] American leaders began talking of the "beginning of the end" of the insurgency, with Vice President Cheney claiming that it was in "the last throes."[229]

But optimism again proved premature. Insurgents launched a new wave of attacks, including a car bomb in Hillah which killed 125, and intensified their operations in Anbar province.[230] They began trickling back into Fallujah.[231] While the political process led some Iraqis to abandon the insurgency or diminish their support for it, it had no effect on the foreign jihadists who were assuming an ever greater role.[232] An American military commander described Iraq as "an insurgency that's been hijacked by a terrorist campaign."[233] Suicide bombs — the weapon of choice for the foreign jihadists — began causing more deaths than any other insurgent activity.[234] While the January 2005 election may have shifted some of the "undecideds" toward the government, there was little sign that support for the insurgency was dropping below the level needed to sustain it. Insurgents do not need all or most of the public to support them, but only a foundation of active support and passivity from the rest. Many of those in the Sunni Arab community who diminished their backing for the insurgency following the election did not automatically become active supporters of the Americans.

As 2005 wore on, the insurgents began to believe that victory — defined as an American withdrawal — was attainable within a few years.[235] According to a report from the International Crisis Group:

> . . . the insurgents' perspective has undergone a remarkable evolution. Initially, they perceived and presented the U.S. presence as an enduring one that would be extremely difficult to dislodge; they saw their struggle as a long-term, open-ended jihad, whose success was measured by the very fact that it was taking place. That is no longer the case. Today, the prospect of an outright victory and a swift withdrawal of foreign forces has crystallised.[236]

When the conflict picked back up in the spring, concern about its effect on the U.S. military again surged. The annual risk assessment by the Chairman of the Joint Chiefs of Staff noted that commanders around the world were pressed to meet established standards.[237] Recruiting shortfalls hindered the ability of the Army to undertake a temporary increase which Congress mandated.[238] Concerns were growing that anti-war sentiment in the United States might damage troop morale.[239] Reports surfaced of dissension within the senior ranks of the military, with some officers claiming that the counterinsurgency strategy was not leading to strategic success.[240] The dissidents particularly were worried that large sweeps were not followed up with a long-term troop presence, allowing the insurgents to return soon after the operation ended.[241] By the end of the summer, in fact, U.S. commanders no longer talked of clearing Anbar. Instead, the Marines were content to hold a handful of cities and towns, and to disrupt insurgent activity with periodic strikes.[242] To many officers, this was frighteningly reminiscent of Vietnam. When the Army's 3d Armored Cavalry Regiment replaced the Marines, it was probably the best prepared U.S. unit to deploy to Iraq and worked hard to implement a "clear, hold, and build" approach.[243] This was quite successful, but units which came later were not able to sustain the effort.

By the autumn of 2005, U.S. strategy increasingly left neutralization of home-grown insurgents to Iraqi security forces.[244] As General Casey described it, "our aim is to defeat the terrorists and foreign fighters and to neutralize the insurgency while we progressively transition the counterinsurgency campaign to increasingly capable Iraqi security forces and ministries."[245] Or, in Secretary of State Rice's words, the United States sought to "break the back of the insurgency so that Iraqis can finish it off without large-scale U.S. military help."[246] "In 2006," President Bush stated, "we expect Iraqis will take more and more control of the battle space, and, as they do so, we will need fewer U.S. troops to conduct combat operations around the country."[247] Following the advice of counterinsurgency experts, American forces began to place greater stress on long-term pacification.[248]

When the administration released a document entitled *National Strategy for Victory in Iraq* in November 2005, it defined long-term victory as "an Iraq that has defeated the terrorists and neutralized the insurgency."[249] This distinction between "terrorists" and "insurgents" was important. With public support for involvement in Iraq fading, the administration placed greater emphasis on the relationship of that conflict to the wider struggle with jihadism.[250] "Prevailing in Iraq," the *National Strategy for Victory in Iraq* stated, "will help us win the war on terror."[251] As General Myers explained it, "as soon as we pull out, that would embolden this al-Qai'da organization, their violent extremist techniques, and surely the next 9/11 would be right around the corner."[252] It was, in a sense, a new "domino theory." This meant that the most important enemies in Iraq—and the ones the United States would focus on—were those affiliated with al-Qai'da or the global jihadist movement.

## The Core Conflict Has Changed.

By 2006, the geographic focus of the insurgency had shifted.[253] During the second half of 2005, the most intense fighting was in Tal Afar and the remote regions of Anbar province. In 2006, Baghdad was the heart of the conflict. More ominously, sectarian violence overshadowed resistance to the U.S. occupation, making a unified and stable Iraq seem further away than ever. After discussions with some Sunni Arab insurgent leaders, Iraqi president Jalal Talibani said they "do not think the Americans are the main enemy. They feel threatened by what they call the 'Iranian threat'."[254] Retribution spiraled upward after a grisly February suicide bombing at a Shiite shrine in Samarra.[255] Death squad killings became a nightly occurrence.[256] Sunni militias sprouted while Shiite ones continued to grow.[257] Mixed neighborhoods underwent "ethnic cleansing" as one group or the other moved out or was forced to leave.[258] Over 1,300 Iraqis died in sectarian killing in March alone.

Patience with the coalition dissipated even among Shiites. Cheering mobs, for instance, surrounded a British helicopter downed by insurgents near Basra in May 2006.[259] Hope that Zarqawi's death in June would lessen sectarian violence proved wrong.[260] Within the Shiite community, armed conflict sputtered and raged between the Iranian-backed Supreme Council for Islamic Revolution in Iraq, the followers of Moktada Sadr, and two smaller parties — the Islamic Dawa Party and Al Fadila al Islamiya. In the north, Kurdish and Arab militias clashed. The sectarian militias had begun splintering into radicalized cells, making them even harder to control.[261] By the autumn of 2006, DoD, in a report to Congress, noted that "the core conflict in Iraq [has] changed into a struggle between Sunni and Shi'ia extremists seeking to control key areas in Baghdad, create or protect sectarian enclaves, divert economic resources, and impose their own respective political and religious agendas."[262] Beyond that, Iraq was, as Solomon Moore and Louise Roug phrased it, "a nation of many wars, with the U.S. in the middle."[263] Anthony Shadid of the *Washington Post*—one of the most experienced observers of Iraq—wrote that he was witnessing:

> the final, frenzied maturity of once-inchoate forces unleashed more than three years ago by the invasion. There was civil war-style sectarian killing, its echoes in Lebanon a generation ago. Alongside it were gangland turf battles over money, power and survival; a raft of political parties and their militias fighting a zero-sum game; a raging insurgency; the collapse of authority; social services a chimera; and no way forward for an Iraqi government ordered to act by Americans who themselves are still seen as the final arbiter and, as a result, still depriving that government of legitimacy.[264]

For the U.S. forces, following counterinsurgency sweeps with sustained pacification appeared to be a good idea come too late. A pessimistic Marine intelligence report, for instance, indicated that insurgents had fought U.S. forces to a stalemate in Anbar province which was a test bed for the "clear, hold, build" approach.[265] In August, Iraq security forces and the American military began a long operation (called TOGETHER FORWARD) to clear the capital of insurgents, even shifting forces from other parts of the country.[266] American commanders recognized that Baghdad was the fulcrum of the violence and that if U.S. and Iraqi security forces could not control militia violence there, they could not hope to do so in the rest of the country.[267] But the concentration of security forces in the capital raised concern that the gains made in other parts of Iraq, particularly Anbar, would be lost with fewer American and Iraqi security forces there to prevent a reinfiltration of the guerrillas.[268] While more bravado than reality, the Mujaheddin

Shura Council, an umbrella organization of insurgent groups, declared that it had established an Islamic state in six provinces.[269] At a minimum, this showed the confidence and intent of the insurgents. Despite the offensive, attacks in Baghdad mounted.[270] General Casey warned that he might need additional troops in the capital, possibly by increasing the overall U.S. force level in Iraq.[271] Eventually October became the deadliest month for U.S. troops in 2006.

Critics of U.S. policy argued that the resources devoted to training the Iraqi security forces remained inadequate.[272] The Iraqis had made strides but not enough to allow an American draw-down.[273] Iraqi military units occasionally refused to move outside their home areas.[274] Many remained inept.[275] The Iraqi police were even worse, with reports that up to seventy percent of its members were infiltrated by sectarian militias.[276] Most major construction projects begun by the United States were left unfinished.[277] The Iraqi political leadership was unwilling or unable to rein in the militias.[278] As James Lyons, former commander of the U.S. Pacific Command, phrased it, "It is an unhappy truth that, from the prime minister on down, no one in Iraq's government has so far demonstrated the backbone or grit necessary to bring the insurgency under control."[279] After several months, Operation TOGETHER FORWARD had failed to secure Baghdad.[280] In fact, violence there had escalated. Sadr's Mahdi Army renewed its offensive stance of 2004, briefly taking over the city of Amarah before being forced to withdraw by Iraqi police.[281]

The public in both Iraq and the United States was running out of patience with the existing counter-insurgency strategy. A majority of Iraqis favored an immediate U.S. pullout, apparently believing that this would not worsen the security situation.[282] Fifty-nine percent of Americans opposed continued U.S. involvement.[283] Fifty-six percent believed sending troops to Iraq in the first place was a mistake.[284] Long time supporters of the effort such as Senator John Warner (R-VA) turned pessimistic.[285] The commander of the U.K. forces in Iraq urged that his country withdraw, stating that "our presence exacerbates the security problems."[286] And while the U.S. Army, both the active and reserve component, succeeded in meeting recruitment goals, its equipment was wearing out and its personnel stretched thin.[287] Military leaders were concerned that the conflicts in Iraq and Afghanistan left the Army unable to maintain proficiency at conventional warfighting. Vice Chief of Staff General Richard Cody expressed concern that the United States could eventually have "an army that can only fight a counterinsurgency."[288] Without billions more in funding, General Schoomaker warned in September 2006, the Army could not maintain its existing levels in Iraq and fulfill other global commitments.[289] The bills for the Iraqi counterinsurgency — or more specifically, for undertaking large-scale protracted counterinsurgency with a force not designed for it — were coming due. After nearly three and half years of counterinsurgency, it was a grim time.

**Adjusting Transformation.**

Iraq has reinforced what national security specialists have long known: the United States is adept at counterinsurgency support in a limited role — El Salvador and the Philippines in the 1950s — but faces serious, even debilitating challenges when developing and implementing a comprehensive counterinsurgency strategy for a partner state. Neither the military nor the government as a whole is optimized for the type of integrated, holistic, psychologically astute, intelligence-intensive, and politically focused effort counterinsurgency demands. Protracted conflict with long intervals of little progress, even significant setbacks, are antithetical to American impatience and do not set well with military and political leaders who feel compelled to demonstrate positive results within their assignment cycle or term of office. And despite a background of great cultural diversity, many Americans do not function well in non-Western cultures. In fact, Iraq has reinvigorated the Vietnam-era idea that the United States simply should not undertake counterinsurgency.[290]

Most policymakers, military leaders, and defense analysts, though, believe that American involvement in counterinsurgency is inevitable as the "long war" against jihadism unfolds. Somewhere in the future, America's enemies will undertake insurgency against a U.S. ally or partner. Some contend that the primary threat faced by the United States and other open democracies is a global insurgency composed of a loose network of affiliated national insurgencies and transnational terrorist movements, unified by a common ideology and a set of shared goals.[291] But even if the challenge is only a series of disconnected national insurgencies, it carries immense implications for the U.S. military. "Our experience in the war on terrorism," as the *National Defense Strategy of the United States of America* puts it, "points to the need to reorient our military capabilities to contend with such irregular challenges more effectively."[292] "Irregular warfare," as a DoD study group noted, "will continue to be the smart choice for our opponents."[293]

Of all the forms of irregular warfare, insurgency is the one with the best chance of success. This makes it appealing to America's enemies. It also means that the United States needs a strategy and an organization that can undertake counterinsurgency effectively. Iraq shows how much there is to do. Since 2003, DoD and, to a lesser extent, other agencies of the U.S. Government have grappled with this, undertaking a number of reforms to augment effectiveness at counterinsurgency and other irregular operations. There has been, in a very real sense, an adjustment in the trajectory of defense transformation. This has been driven both by top-down strategic guidance from senior policy-makers and by bottom-up efforts within the military, most of it shaped by Iraq.

One major step was the publication of the 2005 *National Defense Strategy*.[294] This provided an innovative way of conceptualizing threats to American security, dividing them into traditional challenges (state militaries), irregular ones relying primarily on insurgency and terrorism, catastrophic challenges based on WMD, and disruptive challenges derived from break-through technologies. While it is possible to quibble with the words — irregular challenges actually are more "traditional" for the United States than war against state militaries — the idea is important. For the first time in modern American history, irregular challenges were portrayed as something other than a secondary or peripheral concern. This codified an idea that defense thinkers had proposed since the end of the Cold War: American prowess in large scale, conventional war was driving opponents to other forms of conflict. But while it was useful to recognize this, there was a profound flaw in the way it was done. While the document was a defense strategy, it defined enemies by their operational methods rather than the strategies they used. This reflects a deep tradition within the

U. S. military of focusing on operational concerns rather than strategy. As Dr. Antulio Echevarria phrased it, the United States tends to have a "way of battle" focused on successful campaigns rather than a "way of war" which organizes battlefield success for the attainment of political objectives.[295] At its worst, this can lead to operational success which does not bring strategic victory. The 1991 war with Iraq is a stark case. By focusing on enemy operational methods, *The National Defense Strategy* reflected this tendency, leaving open the question as to whether DoD truly had adopted a strategic approach. In Sun Tzu's words, "what is of supreme importance in war is to attack the enemy's strategy."

Still, with Iraq raging (along with Afghanistan and the war on terror in general), irregular conflict had become the driving focus of the American defense establishment. Secretary Rumsfeld reinforced this through a directive which made stability operations a "core U.S. military mission."[296] Stability operations, he instructed, "shall be given priority comparable to combat operations and be explicitly addressed and integrated across all DoD activities including doctrine, organizations, training, education, exercises, materiel, leadership, personnel, facilities, and planning." This was truly a sea change from the old days when operations other than war or low intensity conflict—to include counterinsurgency—were "lesser included contingencies" as the armed forces prepared for conventional war.

The 2006 *Quadrennial Defense Review* adopted and refined these themes.[297] The United States, it noted, was "in the fourth year of a long war, a war that is irregular in nature. The enemies in this war are not traditional conventional military forces but rather dispersed, global terrorist networks that exploit Islam to advance radical political aims."[298] This required the U.S. military to adopt unconventional and indirect approaches of its own and to operate in many locations simultaneously over long periods of time. While not using the words "insurgency" or "counterinsurgency," the QDR did address "irregular warfare." A few weeks later, the new *National Security Strategy of the United States* continued along the same lines— describing an enemy that used a strategy of insurgency, but not using the word "insurgency," instead relying on the more emotive "terror" (which is often part of an insurgent strategy but never its core).[299]

There were probably two reasons for the choice of words in the strategy documents. One was the perception that labeling enemies "insurgents" gives them legitimacy.[300] This was the paradoxical logic at play in the political realm: phrasing designed with the best intent—in this case, sustaining public and congressional support for U.S. involvement in Iraq— complicated the process of developing an effective counterinsurgency strategy. Insurgency is itself a holistic strategy with multiple dimensions. Focusing the American response on a single component, an operational method such as terrorism or irregular warfare, makes it difficult to formulate an equally holistic and multidimensional response—a strategic one. A second reason was the idea that "irregular warfare" was a broader, more encompassing concept than "insurgency," more akin to the 1980s concept of "low intensity conflict." In fact, a major DoD study preparing for the QDR listed insurgency as an "element" of irregular warfare. Unfortunately, this got it backwards—insurgency is a strategy that includes irregular warfare but also includes political, psychological, and even economic dimensions. It is the nonstate version of "unrestricted warfare"—a concept described by members of the Chinese military.[301] As such, it is multidimensional and holistic; armed conflict is only a part, and often not the decisive one. By making insurgency part of irregular warfare rather than the other way around, the Department of Defense kept its focus on armed violence, thus lessening the attention given to insurgency's more important political and psychological components. While a case could be made that some government agency other than the Department of Defense should bear primary responsibility for the political and psychological dimensions of insurgency, none could, or did.

Given clear strategic guidance from the Secretary of Defense to improve capabilities for irregular warfare and stabilization, the U.S. military, particularly the Army, undertook a wide range of programs and reforms. Modularization was the centerpiece. It was intended to allow commanders to package deployable and sustainable brigade sized units for tasks such as counterinsurgency rather than having to make due with maneuver units designed for conventional combat. Such a tailored brigade task force, for instance, might include less fire support and more military police and intelligence. Other force structure and organization changes dealt with Special Forces. In many ways, Special Forces units were the best configured for counterinsurgency. They were flexible, small, had cultural and linguistic training, and were accustomed to working closely with partner militaries. The problem is that it is difficult and time consuming to create more of them. The war on terror required the largest deployment ever of U.S. Special Operations Forces in general—Delta Force, Army Rangers, Navy SEALs, and Army Special Forces. In the face of this, the U.S. Special Operations Command had warned that it might not be able to provide forces to meet the requests of the regional combatant commands.[302] DoD did attempt to augment Special Operations Forces, planning to increase active duty Army Special Forces battalions, Psychological Operations and Civil Affairs by a third; establish a Marine Corps Special Operations Command; and increase the number of SEAL teams.[303] But there was little chance that a counterinsurgency campaign on the scale of Iraq could be left entirely to Special Forces, given their scarcity and extensive involvement in counterterrorism.

Other reforms and new programs also chipped away at irregular warfare. The services were instructed to enhance language and cultural training, increase the number of commissioned and noncommissioned officers seconded to foreign militaries, and expand foreign area officer programs.[304] Counterinsurgency reappeared in the curriculum at the U.S. Military Academy, the Command and General Staff College, the School of Advanced Military Studies, and the Army War College.[305] Unified Quest—the Army's major annual strategic war game—shifted from a focus on conventional warfighting with an insurgency sidebar to counterinsurgency.[306] The Army created an Asymmetric Warfare Group to assess tactics and develop countermeasures.[307] An Army program at Fort Riley began training midlevel officers as advisors to foreign militaries.[308] At Fort Leavenworth, the Foreign Military Studies Office is leading the development of the Human Terrain System to help brigade commanders understand and deal with "human terrain"—the social, ethnographic, cultural, economic, and political factors in which they operate.[309] The National Training Center—the Army's most important unit level training facility—shifted from conventional combat on a "sterile" battlefield to a complex insurgency scenario complete with civilians and all of the other things a unit could expect to find in Iraq. Information technology allowed "virtual immersion" which gave commanders a true "feel" for the situation in Iraq before they deployed.[310] DoD also began exploring technologies which might be useful in counterinsurgency. Counterinsurgency experts long have argued that technology is unimportant in this type of conflict. While it is certainly correct that technology designed to find and destroy a conventional enemy military force had limited application, other types such as nonlethal weapons and robotics do hold promise for difficult tasks such as securing populated areas, preventing infiltration, and avoiding civilian casualties.[311]

The services and the joint community also developed new doctrine for irregular warfare and counterinsurgency. In October 2004, the Army released its first new counterinsurgency field manual in 20 years.[312] This was influenced heavily by the ongoing fighting in Iraq.[313] While the interim manual — which was produced very rapidly in response to requests from the field — relied heavily on Vietnam-style insurgency as a conceptual template, the revised version released in December 2006 pressed beyond this, seeking to incorporate the changes insurgency has undergone since the Cold War. It also sought to unify Army and Marine approaches — another tension made evident in Iraq. The final manual also integrated Army and Marine doctrine. By 2005, the new doctrine was already in use to prepare units for deployment to Iraq. Other doctrinal efforts were also underway. The Marines, for instance, developed "distributed operations" which sought to match the flexibility and adaptability of insurgents and other irregular opponents by the "deliberate use of separation and coordinated, interdependent, tactical actions."[314] To integrate service efforts, the Pentagon created a Joint Operating Concept for Irregular Warfare.[315]

Even government agencies outside DoD made some changes to increase their capability for counterinsurgency. With DoD facing criticism for mismanagement of the reconstruction efforts in Iraq, President Bush formally designated Secretary Rice to lead any future efforts to stabilize and reconstruct nations suffering from war or civil strife.[316] In 2004 the State Department created the Office of the Coordinator for Reconstruction and Stabilization and named Ambassador Carlos Pascual to head it. This was intended to tie together civilian and military efforts during stabilization by creating a government-wide, comprehensive approach, and to prepare in advance of conflicts rather than simply reacting to them.[317] The office was divided into four "blocks," one for early warning and conflict prevention, one for planning, one for technical capabilities and lessons learned, and one for resources and management. Unfortunately, though, the organization's funding was never commensurate with its ambitious mission. Just as the military has difficulty breaking away from its "big war" mentality, the State Department's organizational culture tends to focus on diplomacy rather than the reconstruction or transformation of other states. It also remains hindered by the small size of the Foreign Service.

The U.S. Agency for International Development (USAID) began its own programs to play a role in operations like the ones in Iraq and Afghanistan. USAID had been an integral part of the U.S. counterinsurgency strategy in the 1960s but, stung by the Vietnam experience, it had moved away from this function. After the post-September 11 shifts in American strategy, the agency reversed this. "The US foreign assistance community," wrote Andrew Natsios, former Director of USAID, "is in the midst of the most fundamental shift in policy since the inception of the Marshall Plan at the end of World War II."[318] As part of this, USAID began to include regional stability and counterterrorism among its programmatic priorities.[319] It sought more of a role in security related reconstruction and better coordination with the Department of Defense.[320]

All of this was useful. But is it enough? To answer that, counterinsurgency must be placed in its wider strategic context.

The decision on the part of the United States to engage (or not engage) in counterinsurgency is shaped by several context-specific factors:

- *the nature of the insurgency*; (The United States was more likely to support a regime facing a communist-based insurgency during the Cold War, or a jihadist insurgency today.)

- *location of the insurgency*; (The United States is more likely to undertake counterinsurgency in its historic areas of involvement like Central America or in regions with extensive tangible national interest like the Gulf or Europe.)

- *strategic distractions*; (The United States is more likely to undertake counterinsurgency if it is not involved in any other major conflicts at the time.)

- *personalities and the worldview of the administration in office*; (presidents such as Kennedy, Reagan, George H.W. Bush, and George W. Bush had worldviews which made them more likely to use American power, including military power, to support friendly regimes facing internal threats.)

- and, *the most recent American experience with counterinsurgency.* (The United States is more likely to undertake counterinsurgency if its most recent experience with it was positive — e.g. El Salvador.)

But there is more to it than that. The propensity to consider engagement in counterinsurgency and the form such engagement takes if national leaders opt for it are shaped by the grand strategy in effect at the time. In a broad sense, there is a great deal of consistency in American grand strategy across presidential administrations. The variance that does occur tends to be defined by two variables: the extent of America's engagement in the world, and the form that engagement takes. Neither of those are dyads but, rather, continua. The choice is not between engagement or disengagement, but how engaged to be and whether to engage only in conjunction with other states. This can be visualized by a simple chart:

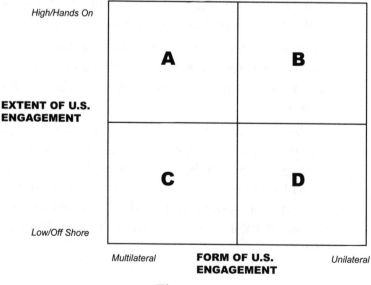

Figure 1.

The actual grand strategy of a presidential administration can fall anywhere on the chart. There are, in other words, a very high number of possibilities (technically even an infinite number). But it makes sense to break the array into four broad options in order to assess the implications for counterinsurgency. For instance, in a "quad A" grand strategy, the United States is willing to become extensively and intensively engaged in the world, but only as part of a multinational coalition. The Clinton strategy was a "quad A" one. In "quad B" the United States is still open to extensive, hands-on engagement, but is willing to do it alone or with a limited number of partners. The George W. Bush grand strategy fits here, as did that of John Kennedy and Lyndon Johnson. It is the "pay any price, bear any burden" quad. In "quad C" the United States will only accept a limited or supporting role in many or most parts of the world, and even then only as part of a coalition. In "quad D" the United States will only accept a secondary or limited role, but might consider doing so on its own or with limited support. The Eisenhower strategy falls here. While there have been no recent instances of "quad C" or "quad D" grand strategies, they cannot be ruled out, particularly if catastrophic terrorist attacks on the homeland raise the costs of global engagement in a significant way or if the United States reaches energy independence, thus lessening the need to manage security in petroleum-producing parts of the world.

What does this mean for counterinsurgency? In simple terms, if future U.S. grand strategy falls in quads C or D, the current reforms—adjusting the trajectory of transformation—are probably adequate. Neither the U.S. Government as a whole nor the military will be optimized for counterinsurgency, but that is acceptable since the nation will only undertake it with partners or in a limited role. In quad A, the current reform *might* be adequate, but there could still be problems with raw numbers if the United States undertakes a major counterinsurgency operation without allies. In other words, the quality issue will be addressed, but not the quantity one. The real problem arises in "quad B." Under such a strategy, current reforms are inadequate, leaving serious shortfalls in both quality and quantity.

If the United States does want an optimized capability for counterinsurgency, what might it look like? While the details of this would require extensive analysis and debate, Iraq and other counterinsurgency campaigns throughout history suggest general characteristics. First, such an organization would need the capacity to undertake three linked but different functions:

- *identifying and preventing insurgencies* by forestalling state collapse and encouraging reform by regimes in danger;

- *preparing for counterinsurgency* by interagency and, possibly, multinational capacity enhancement including strategy development, concept development, technology development, organizational refinement, leader development and education, training, analysis, exercises, and simulations; and,

- *responding to insurgencies* once national leaders decide to engage.

Given this, an optimized U.S. structure for counterinsurgency would have a set of key characteristics.

*Be intelligence-centric.* As Gordon McCormick of the Naval Postgraduate School has pointed out, one of the defining features of insurgency, at least in its early stages, is that the insurgents, which he calls a "force in development," have information dominance (they know the regime's strengths, weaknesses, and locations) but a power shortfall (they do not have the resources to impose their will on the regime). The regime, by contrast, is a "force in being." It has power but an information shortfall (it does not know where or who the insurgents are or, in most cases, what they intend to do).[321] This suggests that the single most vital function for counterinsurgency is augmenting information or, more accurately, knowledge. There is nothing more vital.

*Be fully interagency and, if possible, multinational at every level.* Counterinsurgency succeeds only when there is seamless integration between the political, intelligence, law enforcement, and military efforts. The British experience in Malaya in the 1950s often is considered the classic example. A U.S. organization optimized for counterinsurgency must replicate this at all levels from strategy formulation in Washington to local operations once the United States is involved.

*Be capable of rapid response.* Insurgency is like many pathologies: time matters. It is easier to prevent an insurgency than to defeat one, and it is easier to defeat one early in its lifespan than after it has had time to mature and adapt. If the United States had been prepared to undertake a massive stabilization and reconstruction effort in Iraq in the spring of 2003, the insurgency would never have reached the level that it has. Hence an American organization optimized for counterinsurgency must be able to undertake a range of stabilization, support, and reconstruction actions very quickly. Phrased differently, it must be capable of the stabilization and reconstruction equivalent of "shock and awe." Of course, rapid response is antithetical to the American practice of gradual involvement in counterinsurgency, but that, too, must change if the United States is to be effective. In particular, the United States must have the methods and the resources to restore the security and intelligence services of a failed or failing state quickly. Taking multiple years to stand up a partner military as in Iraq is a recipe for disaster.

*Be capable of sustained, high-level involvement in a protracted operation.* Insurgencies normally last a decade or more. If the United States is to be effective, it must be capable of long-term engagement, crossing presidential administrations, congresses, and the careers of the military and civilian officials who actually undertake the effort. This is difficult but vital. Despite the best efforts, when a unit which had developed local knowledge and contacts is replaced, effectiveness diminishes, at least for a while. "Work arounds" are sub-optimal.

*Be capable of seamless integration with partners.* An American organization optimized for counter-insurgency would be able to work with the militaries, police forces, and intelligence services of a wide range of partners, both those of states actually facing insurgency, and other partners who contribute to the effort. The only way to assure this is to exercise it outside the context of an ongoing insurgency. Ultimately, though, integration and synchronization at the tactical level is much easier than at the policy level. One of the reasons that the United States traditionally has undertaken counterinsurgency support on its own or largely on its own is because it viewed the threat from insurgency differently than other major powers, including allies. If the United States is to optimize for counterinsurgency in the future, that must include extensive diplomatic efforts to align the policy positions of Washington and other major states.

*Be culturally and psychologically adept.* The American organization for counterinsurgency must have organic language and cultural expertise, and be able to augment it rapidly. In particular, it must understand how to shape beliefs, perceptions, and expectations in non-Western cultures, especially those with a "warrior" tradition. This will require revising current thinking and doctrine which assume that the solution to insurgency is building open political systems and economies. That may or may not be true, depending on the cultural context. Moreover, Americans—being Americans—take a "market" approach to insurgency: the side which offers the population the "best deal" wins. Reality, as defined by cultural context, is more complex than that. Sometimes honor, justice, and revenge matter more than schools, roads, and jobs. Counterinsurgent strategists must understand this. An optimized organization must be capable of effects-based planning in an environment with multiple audiences, cultural filters, and great psychological complexity.[322] Its personnel must master the paradoxical logic as it plays out in multiple simultaneous dimensions.

*Be capable of organizational, conceptual and tactical adjustment "on the fly."* As Iraq has demonstrated, insurgencies are deadly "learning contests."[323] A case can be made that the side which learns the quickest and most effectively wins. A U.S. organization optimized for counterinsurgency thus must have rigorous and refined methods for capturing, assessing, and implementing organizational and conceptual changes both as part of its long-term capability enhancement and as part of an ongoing campaign. In addition, it must be capable of regular, critical self-evaluation. Ultimately, the brutal

73

frankness necessary for effective adaptation can work only if there is a mechanism to assess both strategy and operations by experts with no vested professional interest in providing only a positive picture.

In the short term, the greatest shortfalls for an optimized counterinsurgency organization are 1) nonmilitary security forces (something more than local police trained in law enforcement, but less than military units designed for warfighting—in other words, a gendarmerie); 2) surge and expeditionary capacity; 3) capability in nonmilitary functions like political and economic development, plus the creation of functioning police and jurisprudence systems; and, 4) cultural acuity.

Building an optimized system for counterinsurgency within the U.S. Government would be a major undertaking, requiring the creation of new organizations and the stripping of some resources and functions from existing ones. The military would be a major "loser" since it currently owns many of the needed resources. In lieu of major reorganization, the military will retain the dominant role. Hence the United States will continue to approach counterinsurgency as a variant of warfighting. Depending on grand strategy, this may be adequate. Or it may not.

Even a "sub-optimized" organization for counterinsurgency such as the existing one which accords the primary role to the military and lacks some nonmilitary capabilities can and should adopt as many of the characteristics and procedures of a hypothetical optimized one as possible. Take the capability to advise and train a partner security force. The sub-optimized method is to give existing units more training and education, possibly to include recreating the advisers course used during Vietnam. Other elements of the government, including those concerned with policing, jurisprudence, administration, intelligence, and governance, would shift some personnel to counterinsurgency and expand training and educational programs. A similar idea is to create a joint "Stabilization and Reconstruction Command" within DoD with assigned, specialized forces.[324] The optimized method would be to create a special interagency corps with this as a primary mission. Army Special Forces might need to split into separate components, one for direct action and one to provide training and advice to allies. The same holds for intelligence. The sub-optimized method would be to add the ability of existing intelligence personnel to do the type of cross cultural, psychologically complex social mapping activity needed for counterinsurgency. The optimized method would be to create an interagency corps that specializes in this. In terms of having a mechanism for providing senior leaders and policymakers with a regular, objective assessment of the campaign, the sub-optimized method would make use of informal or special assessments from trusted experts. Examples include General Gary Luck's report to Secretary Rumsfeld after a January 2005 trip to Iraq and the June 2005 assessment which retired General Barry McCaffrey undertook for CENTCOM.[325] An optimized solution would be to create a permanent assessment organization for counterinsurgency or stabilization operations composed of a full-time professional core which would then create teams of senior level experts to provide regular, frank analysis during the conduct of a campaign and on U.S. preparations and readiness for this type of activity. Ultimately the key question is whether counterinsurgency plays such a paramount role in American strategy that the costs of optimization are worthwhile, or whether counterinsurgency plays an important but not a dominant role in the strategy, thus implying that a sub-optimized but more effective organization is acceptable.

## Transcending Counterinsurgency.

Counterinsurgency might not be the best response to insurgency. Over the past fifty years, the concept of counterinsurgency has become so encumbered with implications and "lessons," many of them derived from the Cold War, that it is time to move beyond it. At the beginning of the Cold War, insurgents gained the upper hand in part because the regimes they faced, whether indigenous ones or colonial rulers, were ignorant, weak, or inept. But insurgency also succeeded because it was new—regimes simply did not know how to respond to a holistic, political, and psychologically-based strategy which used violence but did not rely on it for ultimate victory. The psychological and political domains were decisive; violence only mattered to the degree that it had psychological and political effects. This was the right strategy for a world of ideological division, the collapse of the European imperial world order, and the political awakening of formerly passive populations. Eventually, though, counterinsurgents came to understand their enemy. They caught up. They understood that counterinsurgency too must be holistic, political, and psychological. By the end of the Cold War insurgency—at least the form of it based on Maoist Peoples' War—was no longer the dangerous force that it had been.

But insurgency did not die, it simply slumbered and evolved. Today, the "cutting edge," paradigm-establishing insurgencies are the ones in Palestine—

and Iraq.[326] In Iraq in particular, most of the insurgent factions seem to realize that they are unlikely to follow the Maoist model and become increasingly "state like," undertake the administration of "liberated areas" and move from terrorism and guerrilla war to conventional military operations. (The Palestinian insurgents do, of course, administer "liberated areas.") While all insurgents must both weaken the regime and then fill the power vacuum, in the Maoist model, the two functions overlap. The insurgents do both simultaneously. 21st century insurgencies approach the functions sequentially, perhaps not out of preference but out of necessity. While the Iraq insurgency has attempted political mobilization and the creation of united fronts and liberated zones in the Maoist tradition, they have largely failed. All that the various elements of the Iraqi insurgency agree on at this point is the destruction of the existing order. "Iraqi model" insurgencies, then, pursue mayhem based on terrorism. Moreover, contemporary insurgencies, particularly "Iraqi model" ones, are even more adept than their forebears at manipulating the psychological effects of violence. Many of the armed actions of Cold War era insurgencies took place in isolated areas, so the psychological and political impact was limited to audiences in the immediate vicinity. Now with the Internet, satellite television networks, and cheap digital video cameras, the audience for insurgent violence is immediate and extensive. Even more than in the past, contemporary insurgency is "armed theater." In addition, modern insurgency is shaped by the role of third and fourth forces. In Iraq, for instance, criminal gangs have worked with the insurgents on kidnappings, killings, and sabotage. Sectarian militias and death squads shape the conflict. The international media — whether intentionally or not—amplify insurgent psychological operations. But American counterinsurgency strategy and doctrine have not addressed the important role of third and fourth forces. It does not indicate how to think about them or what to do with them.

Few modern insurgencies rely on state sponsors. They must either develop alliances with organized crime—again, third forces play a vital role—or undertake criminal activity and other forms of fund raising themselves. Or both. In fact, modern insurgents have shown themselves extremely clever at manipulating a range of tools such as hijacking charities, coercive "taxation," and voluntary contributions from expatriate communities and other sympathetic groups. The collection jars in Boston bars for Irish terrorists are not simply legends. Finally, today's insurgents differ from past ones through possession of what might be called "force projection" capability via terrorism. When the United States undertook counterinsurgency in Vietnam or El Salvador, there was little the rebels could do to strike directly at America. Today's insurgents or, at least, tomorrow's, can. The United States might view counterinsurgency very differently if engaging it inspired sustained terrorism within the American homeland.

The changing nature of insurgency, the coalescence of a transnational (if not global) insurgent alliance, the development of power projection capability by insurgents, the need to address the root causes of insurgency, and the continued holistic, political, and psychological nature of the insurgent threat all suggest that the United States should begin to move beyond the concept of counterinsurgency. It has several conceptual limitations. First of all, it is seen as primarily something that the military does with some support from other agencies. Iraq—like many other insurgencies in history—suggests that a military-dominated approach to counterinsurgency seldom if ever works. If anything, the contemporary security environment, with its information saturation, has amplified this. Second, the concept of counterinsurgency cedes the strategic initiative to the insurgents. Actions by the United States and its partners simply counter what the insurgents do. Third, the word counterinsurgency is simply too tied to the Cold War. It invariably evokes images of Vietnam and thus leads military and political leaders as well as strategic analysts to assume that what worked against Cold War era insurgencies will work against contemporary ones.

Ultimately, "counterinsurgency" should be replaced in the American strategy by the more encompassing concept of "stabilization and transformation."[327] This would help clarify several important points. First, it suggests that the goal is not simply to counter the insurgents, but to attain strategic success defined as the transformation of a problematic state or region, and amelioration of the root causes of the conflict. "Stabilization" does not mean sustaining the political and economic status quo but creating an environment in which they can be altered through non-violent means. Second, the phrase "stabilization and transformation" suggests the necessary sequencing. Stabilization secures political and psychological "space" for transformation. It is necessary for ultimate strategic success but does not, in itself, constitute strategic success (at least not under current U.S. grand strategy). In Larry's Diamond's astute phrase, "we cannot get to Jefferson and Madison without going through Thomas Hobbes."[328] Before there is *open* government, in other words, there must be *effective* government able to assure basic public order.

Third, the phrase "stabilization and transformation" suggests that the military is an important participant but not always the leading one. Clearly stabilizing a state in conflict is something that the U.S. military can and should dominate. But transformation—solidifying strategic success—is a task where the military should be a supporting rather than a supported organization. The military perfectly understands this—even old counterinsurgency doctrine makes note of it. But the message has not resonated beyond the military among those who have the power to enact change. If instead of *counterinsurgency* the United States were undertaking *stabilization and transformation*, both Congress and the Executive would be forced to address capability shortfalls outside the military. Finally, "stabilization" suggests to the U.S. military and to other government agencies that it is not *just* insurgents that must be eliminated or controlled, but violent "third force" groups as well. A fragile regime left facing militias or powerful criminal gangs—or dependent on security contractors—is vulnerable to renewed insurgency or centrifugal forces that undermine effective governance. This also constitutes a strategic defeat or, at best, a badly flawed victory. The term "counterinsurgency" thus has outlived its usefulness.

Iraq has shown the United States that the "one size fits all" approach to insurgency, which is codified in joint and service doctrine, no longer works in the modern world. Sometimes insurgency is as doctrine describes—an attempt by a revolutionary organization to overthrow a constituted government. But other times it is not. As the United States has seen in Iraq, constituting a government rather than supporting a constituted government is the immediate objective. Old style information operations are ineffective in an environment where fourth forces and information saturation dominate. It was not that the United States did not try hard enough in Iraq do dominate the psychological and political battlespaces, but rather that it was not conceptually equipped for 21st century information war. Dealing with third and fourth forces make for a different type of conflict and require a different strategy for which existing doctrine is little help. And, joint and service doctrine for counterinsurgency is based on the construct by which the United States supports a friendly regime facing a violent insurgency. Iraq showed that protracted conflict resulting from outside intervention to change a regime or stabilize a failed state has different strategic, operational, and psychological dynamics. One size does not fit all.

America's counterinsurgency strategy during the Cold War was based on providing assistance and advice until a beleaguered partner regime no longer needed help. After Vietnam, strategy and doctrine stated that this would be done in a supporting rather than leading role. The Iraq conflict did not fit that pattern: the United States had to create a government and economy rather than buttress an existing one. But because the problem looked something like classic counterinsurgency, existing strategy and doctrine were applied.[329] There is an old saying that goes, "when all you have is a hammer, the entire world looks like a nail." That applies to Iraq. Internal conflict resulting from intervention has different dynamics than internal conflict caused by the eroding legitimacy of the existing government, but the United States did not have a strategy or doctrine for post-intervention conflict. Iraq suggests that rather than attempting to approach all internal wars within the framework of counterinsurgency, the United States needs a broader strategy and doctrine for stabilization and transformation which would include classic counterinsurgency as well as other types of internal conflict, including post-intervention warfare and state failure. The strategy for post-intervention or post-state failure conflict should consist of three phases:

- *Intervention.* This should include overwhelming force and massive reconstruction and assistance support.

- *Stabilization.* This is a time of transition when local security forces are not able to stand on their own but the U.S. military role is greatly diminished. Other state militaries and constabularies should play a major role here. In other words, the U.S. hands over stabilization to a multinational force which serves as a bridge between intervention and stabilization under the control of the host nation.

- *Hand over.* This comes when the local security forces are able to assume greater responsibility for security, eventually leading to a withdrawal of all foreign forces except for trainers and advisers.

Based on the Iraq experience, American policymakers should consider a non-U.S. "bridge" force essential rather than simply desirable. In most cases, if there is little prospect of developing a bridge force, the United States should avoid intervention. History, including the ongoing conflict in Iraq, suggests that counterinsurgency support and regime removal can, if necessary, be done unilaterally or nearly unilaterally, but state transformation following regime removal or state failure can only succeed with a broad coalition.

This will always require the tacit or explicit approval of the United Nations.

## A Strategic After Action Review.

The United States could have approached Iraq in one of three ways: as a liberated nation, quickly creating a transitional Iraqi government and giving it sovereignty; as a defeated nation which would have required a massive and long-term occupation like that of Germany and Japan after World War II; or as a failed state which could have been addressed by passing control to the United Nations. Each would have had political disadvantages or significant costs, but each would have avoided entangling the United States in a protracted counterinsurgency campaign. By splitting the difference among them rather than committing to one, the United States became a half-hearted occupier, inspiring armed resistance without deterring it.

Insurgency is a strategy sometimes adopted by the weaker party in an internal war. The war itself can be based on ideology, class, religion, ethnicity, sectionalism, or, most commonly, some combination of these factors. The response—the counterinsurgency strategy—must not be based solely on the fact that the enemy has adopted insurgency, but also on the fundamental cause and form of the conflict. A political conflict—like the one in El Salvador in the 1980s—has different dynamics (and solutions) than a cultural one based on ethnicity or religion. In a political struggle, the insurgents must create a new identity structure and attract supporters to it. Hence the conflict is a competition for "hearts and minds." Advantage accrues to the side which creates the more appealing identity structure (although this may not automatically lead to victory in the absence of security). In a cultural struggle, identity structures already exist. "Hearts and minds" are not subject to competition. Defeating the insurgents comes from empowering a non-insurgent elite within the existing ethnic or religious group, or from imposing the will of the state on the entire group — a negotiated power sharing arrangement or outright defeat. But the "market" based approach which lies at the core of American thinking about counterinsurgency is seldom if ever effective.

The United States also faced another problem: history suggests that outside forces in insurgencies can strengthen their local allies — whether revolutionaries or counter-revolutionaries — but they cannot create them. The United States sought to create the forces of democracy and moderation, not simply strengthen existing ones. Outside jihadists, on the other hand, had only to strengthen preexisting jihadist and anti-American forces rather than create them from scratch. This was a much easier task. Applying existing counterinsurgency strategy and doctrine, derived from 20th century ideological conflict, to Iraq thus was pounding a round peg in a square hole. This hamstrung the effort from the beginning. And it led to the flawed assumption that Iraq's Sunni Arabs would accept a role in a Shiite dominated state if they were protected by constitutional guarantees. American strategy was based on the belief that a functioning constitutional, multi-party democracy was the top priority for all Iraqis except a small number of extremists when, in fact, the security and power of their sect and ethnic group mattered more to a significant number, perhaps most.

Conflicts exist within and can only be understood as part of a historical-strategic context. In Iraq the United States did precisely what it did in Vietnam:

misunderstood the wider historical-strategic context. Americans saw both struggles as one of democracy and freedom versus oppression. The people of Vietnam and Iraq, though, considered their conflict a struggle against Western domination. Many, probably most Iraqis saw the anti-American violence as part of a centuries-long effort by Muslims, particularly Arabs, to resist Western influence, not as something designed to stop democracy and freedom. The dissonance between the way Iraqis saw the conflict and the way Americans saw it hindered the development of effective strategy. And like many insurgencies which begin as resistance to outside influence, the one in Iraq eventually shifted to an internal, sectarian one. This is a very common pattern.

However laudable the overarching American objectives in Iraq, the United States was strategically and conceptually unprepared to realize them. We used flawed strategic assumptions, did not plan adequately, and had a doctrinal void. We had enough force on the ground to antagonize Iraqis or give them the false expectation of security, but not enough to control the Sunni Arab areas. We stayed long enough to be viewed as occupiers but did not administer the country long enough to permanently alter a political culture based on sectarian suspicion, corruption and violence. We created an organization to unify all governmental efforts but did not give it the authority or resources to do so, thus leaving everyone concerned believing that others would do more than they did. Or could. Most of all, American strategy was characterized by a pervasive means/ends mismatch. We sought to alter history, to undertake one of the most profound political, economic, and social transformations in recent history, but we did not allocate money, time, and people in proportion to this ambitious goal.

Ultimately, there are two broad approaches to war. The "scalpel" uses armed force in conjunction with other elements of power to convince an opponent to accept an outcome which it does not want. The "cudgel" simply imposes one's will on an enemy rather than convincing it to make certain desired decisions. From the first approach grows various forms of limited war; from the second, total war. By definition limited war entails fewer costs and risks, and thus is preferable. But it is also less likely than total war to result in a permanently decisive outcome. The grand compromise between the two is a strategy which attempts limited war but is willing and able to shift to total war if the limited approach fails. This willingness was missing in Iraq. The insurgents knew that every instinct of the United States was toward less involvement, not more. They believed their tolerance for violence surpassed America's will to escalate. In reality, that may have been true. It is possible that the highly decentralized structure of the Iraq insurgency rendered it incapable of making strategic calculations and thus unable to react to the fear of escalation. But by signaling in advance that we would go so far and no further, by taking escalation off the table in the insurgency's early months, we made it easier for the insurgents to convince themselves and their supporters that their ability to weather punishment outstripped the willingness of the United States to impose it.

The paradoxical logic haunts the American effort in Iraq at the grand strategic level. The United States was not prepared to mount a rapid, holistic, and effective counterinsurgency campaign, but also was unwilling to write Iraq off before being drawn deep into counterinsurgency as President Clinton did with Somalia. This gave the Iraqi insurgents and, more importantly, other enemies of the United States the impression that insurgency can work. During the Cold War, insurgent success in China, Vietnam, Algeria, and Cuba spawned emulators. While not all of them succeeded, they did try. That is likely to happen again. By failing to prepare for counterinsurgency in Iraq and by failing to avoid it, the United States has increased the chances of facing it again in the near future.

From the beginning, the United States effort in Iraq was hindered by a strategy that did not approach stabilization and transformation as sequential. Ambassador Bremer embraced transformation, seeking to open governance and free markets in a society without the most basic level of security. Not only were the two not properly sequenced, they were antithetical. Some of the most important elements of transformation—de-Ba'athification, dissolving the old Iraq army, and the privatization of state owned industry—contributed to instability by taking away the status and livelihood of thousands of angry men, most experienced in the ways of violence. With hindsight, the United States should have anticipated the security problems, focused all energy on them, and postponed transformation until there was a reasonable degree of stability.

The question of sequencing has another element. The changes to U.S. strategy applied by General Casey and others to a large extent reflected what experts like Kalev Sepp call "best practices" in counterinsurgency.[330] But in this mode of conflict, doing the right thing too late does not work. By the 1970s, the U.S. military and other elements of the government had largely discovered how the insurgency in Vietnam worked and applied fairly successful countermeasures. But politically and psychologically, it was too late, both for the Vietnamese and the American people. Much more so than in conventional war, an insurgency reaches a point of psychological "set" fairly quickly. Once it is set, it is very difficult, perhaps even impossible to reverse.

The counterinsurgency effort in Iraq was made complex by its linkage to the global war on terror. The strategic logic was Napoleonic—draw the enemy into a decisive battle where it can be defeated. Iraq was to be that epic battle of the war on terrorism. Ironically, the defeat of Robert E. Lee in the American Civil War after a long string of victories in seemingly decisive battles discredited the Napoleonic approach for conventional war, but it still held appeal in the most unconventional of global wars which pits the United States against the radical jihadist movement. Future historians may see Iraq as more the strategic equivalent of Gettysburg, Verdun, or Dien Bien Phu. In these battles, military forces established an enclave deep in enemy territory, hoping the opponent would destroy itself trying to reverse the incursion. In Iraq, however, it was not a case of the United States being dug in and the jihadists not. Both openly competed for the same space, thus obviating the enclave method.

Linking the conflict in Iraq to the global war on terror amplified its strategic significance. Paradoxically, this increased public support but constrained strategic flexibility. One reason that the United States succeeded at counterinsurgency in El Salvador was because the stakes were relatively low. Losing there would not have been an irreparable disaster. This meant that Washington had leverage over its allies because it could credibly threaten to write them off. Hence the Salvadorans took their counterinsurgency campaign and the political reforms needed to make it work very seriously. In Vietnam, by contrast, the U.S. attached immense symbolic importance to the struggle. This limited American leverage over the South Vietnamese regime and left the United States unwilling to withdraw even when involvement passed the point where its costs and risks outweighed any possible strategic gains. The basic logic of strategy — that expected gains must be equal to or greater than expected costs and risks — was skewed. Placing Iraq within the context of the war on terror may have done the same.

Given the strategic problems and political imperatives which shaped American involvement in Iraq, it may not be a true test of the ability of the Army or the U.S. military in general to succeed at counterinsurgency. A sound argument can be made that nothing the military could have done would have led to a speedy stabilization of Iraq and its transformation into a free market democracy. But in some ways the military and CPA made the bad hand they were dealt worse. Since counterinsurgency is won or lost in the psychological domain — it is about shaping perceptions, beliefs, and expectations — the first thing a counterinsurgent needs is "situational awareness." The counterinsurgent must know how it is perceived now in order to craft a strategy to create the perception that it wants. The Americans in Iraq never developed such situational awareness during those crucial first few months. They did not ask hard questions about how they were perceived, but simply assumed that the way they wanted to be perceived was reality. And the counterinsurgency campaign, at least during the first year, focused on eliminating insurgents rather than altering perceptions, beliefs, and expectations. The United States, in other words, reverted to a strategy of attrition. The question is whether the U.S. military can, in future counterinsurgencies, develop and implement a different strategy. Is that method too deeply ingrained in its organizational psyche? Can a warfighter be other than a warfighter? Can the military be weaned from this approach through education and leadership? If not, the development and management of America's counterinsurgency campaigns must be ceded to other organizations.

Where does Iraq go from here? At this point, the best feasible outcome is, as Ambassador Dennis Ross describes it, "a central government with limited powers; provincial governments with extensive autonomy; sharing of oil revenue; and, at the local level, some rough form of representation and tolerance for minorities."[331] Equally likely is sustained mayhem which eventually leads the government to settle with the insurgents, potentially giving them control of all or part of the Sunni triangle or at least some degree of political influence. It is possible, though, that the insurgents may provoke the government into a draconian response which might, in turn, lead to intervention by other predominantly Sunni Arab states, thus turning Iraq's civil war into an international one. Either may result in a weak central government, dominated by corruption, with criminal gangs and sectarian militias wielding great influence, or a new authoritarian strong man. Sustaining a multiethnic and multisectarian democracy in the face of mounting sectarian war may be impossible. Outside forces, as Fareed Zakaria notes, can do little to stop a full-blown civil war until its energy is expended.[332] Division of the country into three parts may be inevitable with continued conflict in areas of sectarian overlap, particularly Baghdad and Mosul.

But whether Iraq ultimately turns into a success or failure, it is invaluable as illumination for American strategy. If it is a unique occurrence, then once it is settled, the U.S. military can return to its old, conventionally-focused trajectory of transformation. But if Iraq is a portent of the future, if protracted, ambiguous, irregular conflicts that are cross-cultural, and psychologically complex are to be the primary mission of the future American military (and the other, equally important parts of the U.S. security organization), then serious change must begin.

## ENDNOTES

1. For instance, Vice President Richard Cheney, interviewed by Tim Russert on "Meet the Press," March 27, 2003; and Deputy Secretary of Defense Paul Wolfowitz, remarks as delivered to the Veterans of Foreign Wars, Washington, DC, March 11, 2003.

2. I drove through Baghdad, Umm Qasr, and Basra in late April and May 2003. While we were vigilant and the military officers in our group had side arms, we did not feel particularly threatened.

3. See Ahmed Hashim, *Insurgency and Counter-Insurgency in Iraq*, Ithaca, NY: Cornell University Press, 2006, pp. 24-28.

4. Accounts of who fired first are conflicting. See Ian Fisher, "U.S. Force Said To Kill 15 Iraqis During an Anti-American Rally," *New York Times*, April 30, 2003, p. 1.

5. Scott Wilson, "U.S. Forces Kill Two More Civilians," *Washington Post*, May 1, 2003, p. 1.

6. Rajiv Chandrasekaran and Scott Wilson, "Iraqi City Simmers With New Attack," *Washington Post*, May 2, 2003, p. 21. While reports differ on exactly what happened, it is likely that Iraqis tied to the former regime, incited the Americans to fire into the crowd. Thomas E. Ricks, *Fiasco: The American Military Adventure in Iraq*, New York: Penguin, 2006, p. 139.

7. Susan Sachs, "Two More Servicemen Killed In New Attacks in Baghdad," *New York Times*, May 9, 2003, p. A15; "Two Soldiers Killed in Attacks in Baghdad," *Los Angeles Times*, May 9, 2003, p. A22.

8. Anthony Shadid, "Two U.S. Soldiers Killed in Restive Iraqi City," *Washington Post*, May 28, 2003, p. 1; John Daniszewski and John Hendren, "More Attacks Raise Worries of Violent Resistance in Iraq," *Los Angeles Times*, May 28, 2003, p. 1.

9. William Booth, "Six British Soldiers Killed in Iraqi Town," *Washington Post*, June 25, 2003, p. A1; Neela Banerjee, "Violence In Iraq Spreads," *New York Times*, June 25, 2003, p. A1; Moni Basu, "Basra Quiet Under British, But Discontent Is Building," *Atlanta Journal-Constitution*, June 9, 2003; and, Patrick E. Tyler, "In Iraq's Disorder, the Ayatollahs May Save the Day," *New York Times*, July 6, 2003, p. 4.

10. Anthony Shadid, "In Holy City, Things Are Going Right," *Washington Post*, June 11, 2003, p. A1.

11. Anthony Shadid, "Shiites Denounce Occupation," *Washington Post*, May 19, 2003, p. A1.

12. Amy Waldman, "Cleric Wants Iraqis to Write Constitution," *New York Times*, July 1, 2003, p. A14; Neil MacFarquhar, "In Najaf, a Sudden Anti-U.S. Storm," *New York Times*, July 21, 2003; L. Paul Bremer, *My Year In Iraq: The Struggle to Build a Future of Hope*, New York: Simon and Schuster, 2006, p. 94; Larry Diamond, *Squandered Victory: The American Occupation and the Bungled Effort to Bring Democracy to Iraq*, New York: Henry Holt, 2005, p. 44; and W. Andrew Terrill, *The United States and Iraq's Shiite Clergy: Partners or Adversaries?* Carlisle Barracks, PA: U.S. Army War College Strategic Studies Institute, 2004, p. 11.

13. Illana Ozernoy and Kevin Whitelaw, "Storm Clouds Over Sadr City," *U.S. News and World Report*, May 5, 2003, p. 22; Terrill, *The United States and Iraq's Shiite Clergy*, pp. 16-22; and Bremer, *My Year In Iraq*, pp. 121-136.

14. "Iraq: Seasoned Guerrillas Likely Not Behind Postwar Attacks," *Stratfor.com*, June 13, 2003; and Hashim, *Insurgency and Counter-Insurgency in Iraq*, p. 33.

15. Thomas E. Ricks and Rajiv Chandrasekaran, "In Postwar Iraq, the Battle Widens," *Washington Post*, July 7, 2003, p. 1; and Rajiv Chandrasekaran, "Mortar Attacks Multiply in Iraq," *Washington Post*, October 25, 2003, p. A18.

16. Alexei Barrionuevo, "Resistance Groups Attack Iraqis Who Are Helping Coalition Forces," *Wall Street Journal*, June 27, 2003; Peter Finn, "Iraq Ambushes Beset Troops," *Washington Post*, June 27, 2003, p. A20; Scott Peterson, "New Challenge in Iraq: Sabotage," *Christian Science Monitor*, July 3, 2003; and Michael R. Gordon, "Iraqi Saboteurs' Goal: Disrupt the Occupation," *New York Times*, June 28, 2003.

17. Paul Martin, "Saddam Loyalists Ally With Islamists," *Washington Times*, June 17, 2003, p. 1; Scott Johnson, "Unholy Allies," *Newsweek*, June 16, 2003, p. 30; and, Daniel Williams, "Attacks In Iraq Traced to Network," *Washington Post*, June 22, 2003, p. A1.

18. Michael R. Gordon with Douglas Jehl, "Foreign Fighters Add to Resistance in Iraq, U.S. Says," *New York Times*, June 22, 2003.

19. Interviews by the author with U.S. Army Civil Affairs officers, Baghdad, May 2003; Rowan Scarborough, "Loyalists Put Bounty on U.S. Troops," *Washington Times*, June 19, 2003, p. 1; Raymond Bonner and Joel Brinkley, "Latest Attacks Underscore Differing Intelligence Estimates of Strength of Foreign Guerrillas," *New York Times*, October 28, 2003; and John Hendren, "Defense Officials Profiling the New Enemy," *Los Angeles Times*, July 21, 2003, p. 1.

20. For instance, Tom Lasseter, "Grim Signs of Guerrilla War," *Philadelphia Inquirer*, July 2, 2003, p. 1; and "Guerrilla War in Iraq," *Stratfor.com*, June 18, 2003.

21. Donald H. Rumsfeld, prepared testimony for the Senate Armed Services Committee, Washington, DC, July 9, 2003.

22. Major General Raymond Odierno, video news briefing from Baghdad, June 18, 2003. A year later General Odierno reiterated that he did not think the Iraqi resistance constituted an insurgency until about July 2003. Ricks, *Fiasco*, p. 171.

23. "DoD News Briefing — Mr. Di Rita and General Abizaid," U.S. Department of Defense news transcript, July 16, 2003. See also Vernon Loeb, "'Guerrilla' War Acknowledged," *Washington Post*, July 17, 2003, p. 1.

24. Ricks, *Fiasco*, p. 215.

25. Charles Maechling, Jr., "Counterinsurgency: The First Ordeal by Fire," in Michael T. Klare and Peter Kornbluh, eds., *Low Intensity Warfare: Counterinsurgency, Proinsurgency, and Antiterrorism in the Eighties*, New York: Pantheon, 1988, pp. 26-27.

26. Robert B. Asprey, *War in the Shadows: The Guerrilla in History*, New York: William Morrow, 1994, p. 736.

27. See U. Alexis Johnson, "Internal Defense and the Foreign Service," *Foreign Service Journal*, July 1962, pp. 21-22; and, Henry

C. Ramsey, "The Modernization Process and Insurgency," *Foreign Service Journal*, June 1962, pp. 21-23.

28. For a description of this mode of insurgency, see Steven Metz and Raymond Millen, *Insurgency and Counterinsurgency in the 21st Century: Reconceptualizing Threat and Response*, Carlisle Barracks, PA: Strategic Studies Institute, U.S. Army War College, 2004, pp. 8-10.

29. See Susan Marquis, *Unconventional Warfare: Rebuilding U.S. Special Operations Forces*, Washington, DC: Brookings Institution Press, 1997.

30. These organizational fixes were designed to address the broader category of low intensity conflict rather than counterinsurgency specifically. SOCOM generally has given the training and advisory part of its mission less attention than activities involving direct action, counterterrorism, and the conduct of irregular war.

31. Christopher M. Lehman, "Protracted Insurgent Warfare: The Development of an Appropriate U.S. Doctrine," in Richard H. Shultz, Jr., et. al., eds., *Guerrilla Warfare and Counterinsurgency: U.S.-Soviet Policy in the Third World*, Lexington, MA: Lexington Books, 1989, p. 129. The Executive agencies involved resisted many of the programs of the Armed Services Committee. The Department of Defense only appointed the mandated assistant secretary with great reluctance, and the Low Intensity Conflict Board of the National Security Council was never activated.

32. The Army Low-Intensity Proponency Office was headed by a colonel and housed at the Command and General Staff College at Fort Leavenworth. See the description of this organization in *Military Review*, Vol. 71, No. 6, June 1991, pp. 24-25.

33. See the papers by Richard H. Shultz, Jr. and B. Hugh Tovar in Roy Godson, ed., *Intelligence Requirements for the 1990s: Collection, Analysis, Counterintelligence, and Covert Action*, Lexington, MA: Lexington Books, 1989, pp. 165-236.

34. A. J. Bacevich, James D. Hallums, Richard H. White, and Thomas F. Young, American Military Policy in Small Wars: *The Case of El Salvador*, Washington, DC: Pergamon-Brassey's, 1988, p. 1.

35. In reality, that number often was exceeded by capitalizing on loopholes in the legislation.

36. Americas Watch, *El Salvador's Decade of Terror: Human Rights Since the Assassination of Archbishop Romero*, New Haven, CT: Yale University Press, 1991, p. 141.

37. Field Manual (FM) 100-20/Air Force Pamphlet 3-20, *Military Operations in Low Intensity Conflict*, Washington, DC: Headquarters, Departments of the Army and the Air Force, December 5, 1990, p. 1-5. See also Stephen T. Hosmer, *The Army's Role in Counterinsurgency and Insurgency*, Santa Monica, CA: RAND Corporation, 1990.

38. FM 100-20, 1990, p. 2-18.

39. FM 90-8, *Counterguerrilla Operations*, Washington, DC: Headquarters, Department of the Army, August 1986, p. 1-6.

40. The only major exception was Colombia, more because of the linkage of the insurgency to the drug trade than the strategic significance of the insurgency itself.

41. An important exception was then-Major (currently Lieutenant Colonel) John Nagl who wrote a Ph.D. dissertation at Oxford University which was later published as *Learning to Eat Soup With a Knife: Counterinsurgency Lessons From Malaya and Vietnam*, New York: Praeger, 2002. When the United States became involved in Iraq, this book became very popular within the military and defense communities, and was later released in paperback by the University of Chicago Press.

42. This idea was popularized by Caspar Weinberger, Reagan's Secretary of Defense, and Colin Powell who served as one of Reagan's National Security Advisers and Chairman of the Joint Chiefs of Staff under George H. W. Bush and Bill Clinton. Weinberger developed a set of "principles" for the use of force in a November 1984 speech to the National Press Club in Washington, DC. This speech is reprinted in Caspar W. Weinberger, *Fighting For Peace: Seven Critical Years in the Pentagon*, New York: Warner, 1990, pp. 433-445. Powell did not use the word "principles" but expressed similar ideas in "U.S. Forces: Challenges Ahead," *Foreign Affairs*, Vol. 71, No. 5, Winter 1992/1993, pp. 36-41.

43. For detail, see Steven Metz and Douglas V. Johnson II, *Asymmetry and U.S. Military Strategy: Definition, Background, and Strategic Concepts*, Carlisle Barracks, PA: Strategic Studies Institute, U.S. Army War College, 2001; and the more recent David L. Buffaloe, *Defining Asymmetric Warfare*, Arlington, VA: Association of the United States Army, Institute of Land Warfare, 2006.

44. Joint Pub 1, *Joint Warfare of the Armed Forces of the United States*, January 10, 1995, pp. IV-10 through IV-11.

45. The same discussion of symmetrical and asymmetrical actions is included in the *Joint Doctrine Encyclopedia*, July 16, 1997, pp. 668-670; and Joint Pub 3-0, *Doctrine for Joint Operations*, February 1, 1995, p. III-10.

46. Secretary of Defense William S. Cohen, *Report of the Quadrennial Defense Review*, May 1997, Section II.

47. *Transforming Defense: National Security in the 21st Century*, Report of the National Defense Panel, Washington, DC, December 1997, p. 11.

48. For instance, in 1998 CENTRA Technologies formed a blue ribbon panel on asymmetric warfare on a contract from the intelligence community. One workshop, held in December 1998, included Dr. John Hillen, Mr. Richard Kerr, Admiral William Small, USN (Ret.), Professor Martin van Creveld, Lieutenant General Paul Van Riper, USMC (Ret.), and the author.

49. *Joint Vision 2020*, Washington, DC: The Joint Staff, 2000, p. 5.

50. George H. Bush, "A Period of Consequence," speech at the Citadel, Charleston, SC, September 23, 1999.

51. Condoleezza Rice, "Promoting the National Interest," *Foreign Affairs*, Vol. 79, No. 1, January/February 2000, p. 53. For background and assessment on Rice and the other advisers who shaped the Bush national security strategy, see James Mann, *Rise of the Vulcans: A History of Bush's War Cabinet*, New York: Penguin, 2004.

52. President George H. Bush, graduation speech at the U.S. Military Academy, West Point, New York, June 1, 2002.

53. On the conventional campaign in Iraq, see Michael R. Gordon and Bernard E. Trainor, *Cobra II: The Inside Story of the Invasion and Occupation of Iraq*, New York: Pantheon, 2006; Anthony H. Cordesman, *The Iraq War: Strategy, Tactics, and Military Lessons*, Washington, DC: Center for Strategic and International Studies, 2003; John Keegan, *The Iraq War*, London: Hutchinson, 2004; Thomas Donnelly, *Operation Iraqi Freedom: A Strategic Assessment*, Washington, DC: American Enterprise Institute, 2004; and Williamson Murray and Robert H. Scales, Jr., *The Iraq War: A Military History*, Cambridge, MA: Belknap, 2005.

54. John Tierney and Robert F. Worth, "Attacks in Iraq May Be Signals of New Tactics," *New York Times*, August 18, 2003; Daniel Williams and Anthony Shadid, "Saboteurs Hit Iraqi Facilities," *Washington Post*, August 18, 2003, p. A15; and, Daniel Williams, "Sabotage Derails Iraqi Oil Supply," *Washington Post*, August 17, 2003, p. A22.

55. Anthony Shadid, "Attacks Intensify in Western Iraq," *Washington Post*, August 12, 2003, p. 12.

56. Dexter Filkins, "Attacks on G.I.'s in Mosul Rise as Good Will Fades," *New York Times*, November 27, 2003; Nicholas Blanford, "Why Anti-US Attacks Have Spread to Iraq's North," *Christian Science Monitor*, November 28, 2003; Todd Zeranski, "U.S. General Sees 'Sustained Resistance' in Northern Iraqi City," *Bloomberg.com*, November 19, 2003. Petraeus was promoted to lieutenant general after returning from Iraq.

57. Faye Bowers and Howard Lafranchi, "Insurgents' Goal: Damage, But Also Publicity," *Christian Science Monitor*, December 10, 2003.

58. "In Their Own Words: Reading the Iraqi Insurgency," *Middle East Report* No. 50, Brussels: International Crisis Group, 2006, pp. 23-25. Eisenstadt and White explain it in a slightly different way, dividing military operations into counter-coalition, counter-collaboration, counter-mobility, counter-reconstruction, and counter-stability activities. *Assessing Iraq's Sunni Arab Insurgency*, p. 19.

59. For instance, Office for Reconstruction and Humanitarian Affairs, "A Unified Mission Plan for Post Hostilities Iraq," initial working draft, April 21, 2003, p. I-2.

60. Bremer, *My Year in Iraq*, p. 26. Emphasis in original.

61. Interview by the author with Major General James D. Thurman, Director of Operations (C3) and Assistant Chief of Staff for the Combined Forces Land Component Command, Camp Doha, Kuwait, May 2003; Rajiv Chandrasekaran, *Imperial Life in the Emerald City*, New York: Alfred A. Knopf, 2006, pp. 73-75.

62. Quoted in Gordon and Trainor, *Cobra II*, p. 463. The quotation was from a White House interview with Rice by Gordon (Michael Gordon, email correspondence with the author, September 12, 2006).

63. CFLCC OPLAN ECLIPSE II briefing by Colonel Kevin Benson at the Phase IV Conference, Doha, Qatar, May 2003; and,

interview by the author with COL Kevin Benson, Camp Doha, Kuwait, April 2003. For detail on this plan and its development, see Kevin C. M. Benson, "OIF Phase IV: A Planner's Reply to Brigadier Aylwin-Foster," *Military Review*, March-April 2006, Vol. 86, No. 2, pp. 61-68. Colonel Benson was CFLCC's lead planner for Phase IV operations.

64. *Iraq: One Year After*, Report of an Independent Task Force on Post-Conflict Iraq, New York: Council on Foreign Relations, March 2004, p. 15.

65. Gordon and Trainor, *Cobra II*, pp. 457-458.

66. Diamond, *Squandered Victory*, p. 32; Chandrasekaran, *Imperial Life in the Emerald City*, p, 29; and, Niall Ferguson, *Colossus: The Price of America's Empire*, New York: Penguin, 2004, p. 203.

67. Gordon and Trainor, *Cobra II*, p. 459.

68. President George H. Bush, remarks at the U.S. Naval Academy Commencement, Annapolis, MD, May 25, 2001.

69. Max Boot, "The New American Way of War," *Foreign Affairs*, Vol. 82, No. 4, July/August 2003, p. 42.

70. James Kitfield, *War and Destiny: How the Bush Revolution in Foreign and Military Affairs Redefined American Power*, Washington, DC: Potomac, 2005, pp. 26-32; Steven Metz, "The American Experience With Defence Transformation," *Defence Studies*, Vol. 6, No. 1, March 2006, pp. 1-25; and Frederick Kagan, *Finding The Target: The Transformation of American Military Policy*, New York: Encounter, 2006, pp. 287-322.

71. Secretary Rumsfeld, interview with Richard Dixon of WAPI-AM Radio, Birmingham, AL, September 28, 2004.

72. David H. Petraeus, "Learning Counterinsurgency: Observations From Soldiering in Iraq," *Military Review*, Vol. 86, No. 4, January-February 2006, p. 2.

73. Nigel Aylwin-Foster, "Changing the Army for Counterinsurgency Operations," *Military Review*, Vol. 85, No. 6, November-December 2005, p. 9.

74. Isaiah Wilson, "Thinking Beyond War: Civil-Military Operational Planning in Northern Iraq," paper prepared for delivery at the Annual Meeting of the American Political Science Association, Chicago, IL, September 2-5, 2004, p. 15.

75. The Operation IRAQI FREEDOM after action report of the Third Infantry Division (Mechanized), for example, admits that the unit did not have a fully developed plan for the transition to stabilization and support operations (p. 17). This undoubtedly held for others as well.

76. Email correspondence with the author, June 2004.

77. *Ibid.*

78. Michael Kilian, "Areas Bypassed in War Are Problem, Rumsfeld Explains," *Chicago Tribune*, June 19, 2003.

79. Chandrasekaran, *Imperial Life in the Emerald City*, pp, 28-37; and George Packer, *The Assassins' Gate: America In Iraq*, New York: Farrar, Straus, and Giroux, 2005, pp. 120-135.

80. Ariana Eunjung Cha, "In Iraq, the Job of a Lifetime," *Washington Post*, May 23, 2004, p. A1; and Rajiv Chandrasekaran, "Ties to GOP Trumped Know-How Among Staff Sent to Rebuild Iraq," *Washington Post*, September 17, 2006. For detail, see Chandrasekaran, *Imperial Life in the Emerald City*.

81. This was reinforced in discussions the author held with ORHA personnel in Baghdad, May 2003, and multiple email interviews with brigade and battalion commanders and staff officers who served in Iraq from 2003 to 2004. See also Joshua Hammer and Colin Soloway, "Who's In Charge Here?" *Newsweek*, May 26, 2003, p. 28; Ricks, *Fiasco*, pp. 179-183, 209-212; and, Rajiv Chandrasekaran, "Mistakes Loom Large as Handover Nears," *Washington Post*, June 20, 2004, p. A1.

82. Lieutenant Colonel Glenn Patten, chief, Phase IV plans, CFLCC, interview with the author, Baghdad, May 12, 2003. For detail, see Colonel Paul F. Dicker, "Effectiveness of Stability Operations During the Initial Implementation of the Transition Phase for Operation Iraqi Freedom," U.S. Army War College, Strategy Research Project, Carlisle Barracks, PA, March 19, 2004.

83. Quoted in Timothy Carney, "We're Getting In Our Own Way," *Washington Post*, June 22, 2003, p. B1. Ambassador Carney was a senior member of the ORHA/CPA staff. The arrival of Ambassador Bremer in May 2003 and the reorganization of ORHA into the CPA did not resolve the civil-military problems. See Rajiv Chandrasekaran, "Who Killed Iraq?" *Foreign Policy*, No. 156, September/October, 2006, pp. 36-43; and Sharon Behn, "General Assails CPA Bureaucracy as Unresponsive," *Washington Times*, July 1, 2004, p. 1.

84. S3 from the 1st Infantry Division, email correspondence with the author, June 2004.

85. Email correspondence with the author, June 2004.

86. CPA did move forward on strategic and operational planning after the arrival of L. Paul Bremer in May 2003. See Andrew Rathmell, "Planning Post-Conflict Reconstruction in Iraq: What Can We Learn?" *International Affairs*, Vol. 81, No. 5, October 2005, pp. 1026-1030. Rathmell served on the CPA staff.

87. Peter Slevin, "Hussein Loyalists Blamed for Chaos," *Washington Post*, May 15, 2003, p. 1.

88. Secretary of Defense Donald H. Rumsfeld, interview with Todd McDermott, WCBS-TV, New York City, May 27, 2003.

89. DoD news briefing from the Pentagon, Washington, DC, May 20, 2003.

90. Ambassador Paul Bremer, video news briefing from Baghdad on post-war reconstruction and stabilization efforts, June 12, 2003; and Lieutenant General David McKiernan, Coalition Joint Task Force (CJTF) 7 Commander, video news briefing from Baghdad, June 13, 2003. CJTF 7 had replaced CFLCC as the primary military headquarters in Iraq. McKiernan, who had been the CFLCC commander, initially led CJTF 7 as well.

91. Michael R. Gordon, "U.S. Planning to Regroup Armed Forces in Baghdad, Adding to Military Police," *New York Times*, April 30, 2003.

92. Interview by the author with Lieutenant Colonel John Charlton, battalion commander in the Third Infantry Division, Baghdad, May 3, 2003; interview by the author with Colonel Martin Stanton, Coalition Forces Land Component Command C9 (Civil-Military Affairs Staff Section), Baghdad, May 14, 2003; and Dion Nissenbaum, "Marines Play Awkward Role as a Nation Building Force," *San Jose Mercury News*, May 1, 2003.

93. This is based on the author's observations in and around Baghdad during May 2003, and on correspondence and discussion with a wide range of officers and noncommissioned officers during 2003.

94. Paul Wiseman and Vivienne Walt, "Hostility Toward U.S. Troops Is Running High in Baghdad," *USA Today*, May 7, 2003, p. 1; Edmund L. Andrews and Susan Sachs, "Iraq's Slide Into Lawlessness Squanders Good Will For U.S.," *New York Times*, May

18, 2003, p. 1; Peter S. Goodman, "Angry Iraqis Blame U.S. for Fuel Shortage," *Washington Post*, May 8, 2003, p. E1; Dion Nissenbaum, "Anger in Iraq Grows as U.S. Lags," *Philadelphia Inquirer*, May 12, 2003, p. 1; Esther Schrader and Paul Richter, "U.S. Delays Pullout in Iraq," *Los Angeles Times*, July 15, 2003, p. 1; and John Hendren and Azadeh Moaveni, "Anti-U.S. Sentiment Festers as Order and Calm Prove Elusive," *Los Angeles Times*, May 24, 2003.

95. Maureen Fan, Andrea Gerlin, and Soraya Sarhaddi Nelson, "U.S. Hints at Boost in Forces Amid Iraqi Troubles," *Philadelphia Inquirer*, May 13, 2003; Michael R. Gordon, "Fear of Baghdad Unrest Prompts a Halt in Sending Troops Home," *New York Times*, May 15, 2003; Thomas E. Ricks, "Division Gears Up For Peace," *Washington Post*, May 17, 2003, p. 20; Michael R. Gordon, "Instead of Going Home, G.I.'s Get a New Mission," *New York Times*, June 2, 2003; and, Vernon Loeb and Karen DeYoung, "U.S. to Bolster Security in Iraq," *Washington Post*, May 16, 2003, p. 20.

96. Thomas Ricks, "U.S. Alters Tactics in Baghdad Occupation," *Washington Post*, May 25, 2003, p. 1; Tim Potter, "U.S. Trying to Get Handle on Baghdad's Crime Wave," *Philadelphia Inquirer*, May 18, 2003; Patrick E. Tyler, "U.S. Steps Up Efforts to Curb Baghdad Crime," *New York Times*, May 16, 2003; and, Tom Hundley and E. A. Torriero, "U.S. Boosts Troop Strength in Baghdad to Help Fight Crime," *Chicago Tribune*, May 18, 2003. Garner was particularly critical of the limited presence of American troops during the April and May looting in Baghdad. During a discussion with the author in early May in Baghdad, he complained of having driven through the city for an hour the previous night without seeing an American solider.

97. Daniel Williams, "U.S. Bolsters Forces in Restive Sunni Area," *Washington Post*, June 5, 2003, p. A22.

98. McKiernan, video news briefing of June 13, 2003.

99. Stephen Glain, "In Iraq's North, US Skirts Bureaucracy," *Boston Globe*, June 1, 2003, p. 8; Michael R. Gordon, "101st Airborne Scores Success in Northern Iraq," *New York Times*, September 4, 2003, p. 1; Ricks, *Fiasco*, pp. 228-232; and Robert Hodierne, "A Change of Command in Northern Iraq," *Defense News*, February 9, 2004.

100. Neela Banerjee, "British Tread Carefully in South Iraq," *New York Times*, July 14, 2003.

101. Abizaid quoted in Jim Garamone, "Abizaid: U.S. Displaying 'Offensive' Spirit in Iraq," Armed Forces Information Service, June 25, 2003. On the raids and sweeps, see Michael R. Gordon, "In Major Assault, U.S. Forces Strike Hussein Loyalists," *New York Times*, June 13, 2003; Daniel Williams, "U.S. Stages Raid to Quell Iraqi Attacks," *Washington Post*, June 12, 2003, p. A1; Rajiv Chandrasekaran and Peter Finn, "U.S. Clamps Down on Iraqi Resistance," *Washington Post*, July 1, 2003, p. A1; Daniel Williams, "Fighters' Camp Hit by Major U.S. Strike," *Washington Post*, June 14, 2003, p. A1; Patrick E. Tyler, "As U.S. Fans Out in Iraq, Violence and Death on Rise," *New York Times*, June 14, 2003; David Rohde, "U.S. Forces Launch Raids Across Iraq to Quell Uprisings," *New York Times*, June 15, 2003; Thomas E. Ricks, "U.S. Adopts Aggressive Tactic on Iraqi Fighters," *Washington Post*, July 28, 2003, p. A1; and Edmund L. Andrews, "American Forces Carry Out Raids in Central Iraq," *New York Times*, June 30, 2003.

102. Edward N. Luttwak, *Strategy: The Logic of War and Peace*, Cambridge, MA: Belknap, 1987.

103. David Galula, *Pacification in Algeria, 1956-1958*, Santa Monica, CA: RAND Corporation, 2006 reprint of a 1963 publication, p. 218.

104. Ilene R. Prusher, "U.S. Antiguerrilla Campaign Draws Iraqi Ire," *Christian Science Monitor*, June 16, 2003; Ellen Barry and Bryan Bender, "US Support in Iraq Fades After Raids," *Boston Globe*, June 15, 2003, p. 1; and Ann Scott Tyson, "In Iraq, US Enters Tricky New Phase," *Christian Science Monitor*, June 16, 2003, p. 1.

105. Ken Dilanian and Drew Brown, "U.S. Errors Creating New Enemies in Iraq," *Philadelphia Inquirer*, September 17, 2003, p. 1.

106. *Report Of The International Committee Of The Red Cross On The Treatment By The Coalition Forces Of Prisoners Of War And Other Protected Persons By The Geneva Conventions In Iraq During Arrest, Internment And Interrogation*, February 2004.

107. Quoted in Ricks, *Fiasco*, p. 303.

108. Patrick J. McDonnell, "Army Aims to Achieve Delicate Balance in Iraq," *Los Angeles Times*, July 16, 2003; Vernon Loeb, "Instead of Force, Friendly Persuasion," *Washington Post*, November 5, 2003, p. A24; Mark Mazzetti, "Iraq War 2.0," *U.S. News and World Report*, November 10, 2003; Vernon Loeb, "U.S. Forces Press Attack Against Iraqi Resistance," *Washington Post*,

October 26, 2003, p. A27; David E. Sanger, "Iraq Paradox: Cracking Down While Promoting Freedom," *New York Times*, October 28, 2003; and Patrick J. McDonnell, "U.S. Adopts New Tactics to Counter Iraq Foes," *Los Angeles Times*, September 7, 2003, p. 1;

109. Petraeus, "Learning Counterinsurgency, " p. 5; Michael Toner, "Commander's Emergency Response Program (CERP)," *The Armed Forces Comptroller*, Vol. 49, No. 3, Summer 2004, pp. 30-31; and Mark Martins, "No Small Change of Soldiering: The Commander's Emergency Response Program (CERP) in Iraq and Afghanistan," *Army Lawyer*, February 2004, pp. 1-20.

110. Discussions by the author with a senior Army commander who was in Iraq during 2003.

111. William Booth and Daniel Williams, "U.S. Forces Mix Carrots and Sticks," *Washington Post*, June 16, 2003, p. A18; and, David Rohde, "G.I.'s Offer Carrot of Relief as Well as Stick of Raids," *New York Times*, June 16, 2003.

112. Chandrasekaran, Imperial Life in the Emerald City, p. 78; and, Packer, *The Assassins' Gate*, p. 146.

113. Quoted in Dana Milbank, "U.S. Faces Long Stay in Iraq, Bush Says," *Washington Post*, July 2, 2003, p. A1. During testimony and questioning before the U.S. House of Representatives Committee on Armed Services on June 18, 2003, Deputy Secretary of Defense Paul Wolfowitz did not dispute suggestions that the United States could be in Iraq for as long as a decade.

114. When the author was in Baghdad in mid-May 2003, even Corps headquarters was using un-air conditioned tents, make-shift plywood showers, and slit latrines.

115. Eric Schmitt, "Forces Strained in Iraq Mission, Congress Is Told," *New York Times*, September 19, 2003; and, James Kitfield, "Army Troops, Budget Stretched to the Limit," *National Journal*, September 8, 2003. The military infrastructure issue again illustrated the paradoxical logic: large forward operating bases were built to protect American troops and sustain their morale. But at the same time, this further isolated the troops from the Iraqi public and complicated efforts to build understanding and trust.

116. *An Analysis of the U.S. Military's Ability to Sustain an Occupation of Iraq*, Washington, DC: Congressional Budget Office, September 3, 2003.

117. Thom Shanker and Eric Schmitt, "Army May Reduce Length of Tours in Combat Zones," *New York Times*, September

27, 2004, p. 1; and, Bradley Graham and Dana Milbank, "Many Troops Dissatisfied, Iraq Poll Finds," *Washington Post*, October 16, 2003, p. A1.

118. Thom Shanker, "U.S. to Use Mix of Regular, National Guard and Reserve Troops in Iraq," *New York Times*, July 24, 2003; Joseph L. Galloway, "Army Plans New Guard Call-Up to Relieve Weary Troops in Iraq," *Philadelphia Inquirer*, July 23, 2003; and, Thom Shanker, "Pentagon Says It Will Call Up Added Reserves," *New York Times*, October 22, 2003.

119. Vernon Loeb, "Pentagon Unveils Plan to Bolster Forces in Iraq," *Washington Post*, July 24, 2003, p. A8; and, Vernon Loeb and Steve Vogel, "Reserve Tours Are Extended," *Washington Post*, September 9, 2003, p. A1.

120. The coalition members are listed in the U.S. Department of State's Iraq weekly status report.

121. Esther Schrader, "Foreign Troops Key to Iraq Plans," *Los Angeles Times*, July 25, 2003; Peter Slevin and Bradley Graham, "U.S. Renews Bid to Involve More Nations in Iraq," *Washington Post*, August 21, 2003, p. A1; Peter Slevin, "Policing of Iraq to Stay U.S. Job," *Washington Post*, June 22, 2003, p. 20; Drew Brown, "U.S. Military seeks Help Establishing Peace in Iraq," *Philadelphia Inquirer*, June 22, 2003; David E. Sanger, "Bush Looks to U.N. to Share Burden on Troops in Iraq," *New York Times*, September 3, 2003; and Mike Allen and Vernon Loeb, "U.S. Wants Larger U.N. Role in Iraq," *Washington Post*, September 3, 2003, p. A1.

122. Francis Fukuyama, *America at the Crossroads: Democracy, Power, and the Neoconservative Legacy*, New Haven, CT: Yale University Press, 2006, p. 100

123. See Andrew Rathmell, *et. al., Developing Iraq's Security Sector: The Coalition Provisional Authority's Experience*, Santa Monica, CA: RAND Corporation, 2005; and Anthony H. Cordesman, *Iraqi Force Development: The Challenges of Partnership in Nation-Building*, Washington, DC: Center for Strategic and International Studies, 2005.

124. Coalition Provisional Authority Order Number 22, Creation of a New Iraqi Army, August 7, 2003. See also Rajiv Chandrasekaran, "U.S. to Form New Iraqi Army," *Washington Post*, June 24, 2003, p. A1; and Patrick E. Tyler, "U.S.-British Project: To Build a Postwar Iraqi Armed Force of 40,000 Soldiers in Three Years," *New York Times*, June 24, 2003.

125. Coalition Provisional Authority Order No. 28, Establishment of the Iraqi Civil Defense Corps, September 3, 2003. See also Eric Schmitt, "U.S. Is Creating an Iraqi Militia to Relieve G.I.'s," *New York Times*, July 21, 2003, p. 1; Keith Johnson and Alexi Barrionuevo, "U.S. Declares Local Force Will Police, Patrol Iraq," *Wall Street Journal*, June 26, 2003; and Sameer N. Yacoub, "Training Begins For Iraq's Militia," *Washington Times*, August 16, 2003, p. 5.

126. "Rebuilding Iraq: Preliminary Observations on Challenges in Transferring Security Responsibilities to Iraqi Military and Police," Statement of Joseph A. Christoff, Director of International Affairs and Trade at the Government Accountability Office, submitted to the U.S. House of Representatives Subcommittee on National Security, Emerging Threats, and International Relations on March 14, 2005. At about the same time, CPA also announced an escalated process for the transition to Iraqi self-governance, thus abandoning Ambassador Bremer's notion of a period of extended tutelage while Iraq's mastered the intricacies of democracy.

127. Robin Wright and Thomas E. Ricks, "New Urgency, New Risks in 'Iraqification'," *Washington Post*, November 14, 2003, p. 1; and, David E. Sanger and Eric Schmitt, "Bush In a Hurry to Train Iraqis in Security Duty," *New York Times*, October 30, 2003, p. A1.

128. Peter Grier and Faye Bowers, "The Risks of Rapid 'Iraqification'," *Christian Science Monitor*, November 6, 2003, p. 1.

129. Thom Shanker, "Army Is Designing Ways to Reorganize Its Force," *New York Times*, August 6, 2003; and "New Directions For U.S. Army," *Jane's Defence Weekly*, August 27, 2003.

130. General Richard A. Cody, Vice Chief of Staff of the Army, and Claude M. Bolton Jr., Assistant Secretary of the Army for Acquisition, Logistics and Technology, prepared statement for testimony before the U.S. Senate Committee on Armed Service, Airland Subcommittee, March 15, 2005.

131. U.S. Army 2006 Posture Statement, *A Campaign Quality Army With Joint and Expeditionary Capabilities*, p. 6.

132. Michael O'Hanlon of the Brookings Institution and Frederick Kagan of the American Enterprise Institute have been among the most persistent in calling for an increase in the size of the Army. See, for instance, O'Hanlon's "Breaking the Army," *Washington Post*, July 3, 2003, p. 23; "The Need to Increase the Size of the Deployable Army," *Parameters*, Vol. 34, No. 3, Autumn 2004,

pp. 4-17; and, *Defense Policy for the Post-Saddam Era*, Washington, DC: Brookings Institution, 2005; and Kagan's "The Army We Have: It's Too Small," *Weekly Standard*, December 27, 2004; "Army Needs More Strength in Numbers," *New York Daily News*, August 24, 2006; and "The U.S. Military's Manpower Crisis," *Foreign Affairs*, Vol. 85, No. 4, July/August 2006, pp. 97-110. Other organizations and individuals took a similar line. In January 2005, for instance, the Project for the New American Century sent a letter to leading members of Congress including the number of U.S. ground forces. The signatories included defense experts from both ends of the political spectrum, retired senior military leaders, and former officials of the Clinton and G. H. W. Bush administrations.

133. Mark Sappenfield, "Dueling Views on Army Size: Congress vs. Rumsfeld," *Christian Science Monitor*, May 17, 2005. In early 2004 a bipartisan group of 128 members of the House, led by Heather Wilson (R-NM), called on President Bush to increase the Army's overall size, called end strength, and to reduce the time reservists must spend on active duty. In October 2004 the FY2005 Defense Authorization Act increased Army end strength by 20,000 and Marine Corps end strength by 3,000 for FY2005, with additional increases authorized in future years. For background, see Edward F. Bruner, *Military Forces: What Is the Appropriate Size for the United States?* Congressional Research Service Report for Congress, May 28, 2004. The National Defense Authorization Act for Fiscal Year 2006 (Public Law 109-163) authorized active duty end strength for the Army at 512,400 and 179,000 for the Marine Corps. Additional authority also was provided in section 403 of that Act to increase active duty end strength for the Army by up to 20,000 and increase Marine Corps active duty end strength by up to 5,000 above the fiscal year 2006 authorized levels of 512,400 and 179,000, respectively, during fiscal years 2007 through 2009.

134. Christopher Hellman, "Rumsfeld's Iraq Dilemma," *Defense News*, September 8, 2003, p. 8; Jonathan Landay, "Congress, Rumsfeld at Odds on Army," *Philadelphia Inquirer*, October 26, 2003; and Robert Burns, "Rumsfeld Doesn't Want Military Expansion," *Washington Post*, January 13, 2004.

135. Donald H. Rumsfeld, "New Model Army," *Wall Street Journal*, February 3, 2004.

136. Eric Schmitt, "Rumsfeld Says More G.I.'s Would Not Help In Iraq," *New York Times*, September 11, 2003; and Eric Schmitt,

"General in Iraq Says More G.I.'s Are Not Needed," *New York Times*, August 29, 2003.

137. Ronald Brownstein and Richard Simon, "U.S. Military Strength Called Lacking in Iraq," *Los Angeles Times*, August 25, 2003, p. 1. Ambassador Bremer told National Security Adviser Rice that the Coalition only had about half the number it needed. Bremer, *My Year In Iraq*, p. 106.

138. Neil MacFarquhar, "Rising Tide of Islamic Militants See Iraq as Ultimate Battlefield," *New York Times*, August 13, 2003, p. 1; and, Peter Finn and Susan Schmidt, "Al-Qai'da Plans a Front in Iraq," *Washington Post*, September 7, 2003, p. A1.

139. Rowan Scarborough, "U.S. Commander to Focus on Foreign Terrorists in Iraq," *Washington Times*, August 8, 2003, p. 5; and, Vernon Loeb, "New Enemy May Require New Tactics," *Washington Post*, October 28, 2003, p. A14. Critics such as Ricks in *Fiasco* suggest that this shift may have had less to do with the aggregate importance of the foreigners in the insurgency than to the fact that foreign jihadists tended to use electronic means to communicate while many of the Iraqi groups used informal methods, especially face-to-face contact. This made it easier for U.S. intelligence to find and identify the foreigners.

140. Lieutenant General Ricardo Sanchez, quoted in Tyler Marshall, "U.S. General Says Iraqi Rebels Getting Stronger," *Los Angeles Times*, October 3, 2003, p. A1.

141. Alissa J. Rubin, "Attack Is a Media Coup For Iraq Resistance, Experts Say," *Los Angeles Times*, October 27, 2003, p. 1.

142. Vernon Loeb, "New Enemy May Require New Tactics," *Washington Post*, October 28, 2003, p. A14.

143. Nicholas Blanford, "Attacks Turning to US Allies in Iraq," *Christian Science Monitor*, December 1, 2003, p. 1.

144. Dexter Filkins, "Attacks on G.I.'s in Mosul Rise as Good Will Fades," *New York Times*, November 27, 2003.

145. Christine Spolar, "Iraqi Soldiers Deserting New Army," *Chicago Tribune*, December 9, 2003.

146. Anthony Shadid, "Battle Reveals New Iraqi Tactics," *Washington Post*, December 2, 2003, p. 1.

147. Quoted in Sabah Jerges, "Guerrillas Now 'Stand and Fight'," *Washington Times*, December 2, 2003, p. 13.

148. Journalists quickly drew the comparison to Tet. See, for instance, James Kitfield, "Ramadan Offensive," *National Journal*, November 1, 2003, pp. 3326-3332. Ultimately, though, the Iraq insurgents proved unable to undertake a nation-wide offensive on the scale that the Viet Cong or other more hierarchical insurgents movements were. The loose, networked configuration of the Iraq insurgency made it adaptable and difficult to eradicate, but was an impediment to coordination.

149. Jonathan S. Landay, "CIA Has a Bleak Analysis of Iraq," *Philadelphia Inquirer*, November 12, 2003, p. 1; Douglas Jehl, "C.I.A. Report Suggests Iraqis Are Losing Faith in U.S. Efforts," *New York Times*, November 13, 2003; and, Warren P. Strobel and Jonathan S. Landay, "CIA: Iraq at Risk of Civil War," *Philadelphia Inquirer*, January 22, 2004, p. 1.

150. Bremer, *My Year in Iraq*, p. 221.

151. Doyle McManus and Sonni Efron, "The Iraq Dilemma: Do It Right or Quick?" *Los Angeles Times*, December 28, 2003, p. 1.

152. Michael R. Gordon, "For U.S. Foes, a Major Blow: Fighters Now Lack a Symbol," *New York Times*, December 15, 2003.

153. Rajiv Chandrasekaran, Thomas E. Ricks, and Anthony Shadid, "Belief That Insurgency Will Fade May Be Misplaced," *Washington Post*, December 15, 2003, p. A1.

154. U.S. Army Intelligence and Security Command, Intelligence Operations Center, Terrorism Analysis Summary, January 30, 2004; Patrick J. McDonnell, "Iraqi Insurgency Is as Lethal as Ever Since Hussein's Capture," *Los Angeles Times*, February 4, 2004, p. 1; Thom Shanker and Eric Schmitt, "G.I. Toll Is Rising as Insurgents Try Wilier Bombs and Tactics," *New York Times*, March 15, 2004, p. 1; and, Carol Rosenberg, "Resurgence In Road Bombs Baffles Military," *Miami Herald*, March 16, 2004.

155. Jeffrey Gettelman, "11 Iraqi Police Officers Are Killed by Gunmen," *New York Times*, March 24, 2004; and, Christopher Torchia, "Iraqi Police Targets of Guerrilla Attacks," *Washington Times*, March 26, 2004, p. 19. By September 2006, about 4,000 Iraqi policemen had been killed by the insurgents. John O'Neil, "U.S. General Says 4,000 Iraqi Policemen Have Died in 2 Years," *New York Times*, October 7, 2006.

156. Romesh Ratnesar with Phil Zabreskie, "The Rise of the Jihadists," *Time*, January 26, 2004; and, Hannah Allam and Tom

Pennington, "Troops Battle to Rid Town of Suspected Cell," *Philadelphia Inquirer,* January 23, 2004.

157. Bing West, *No True Glory: A Frontline Account of the Battle for Fallujah,* New York, Bantam: 2005, p. 42.

158. Stephen Schwartz, "Jihadists In Iraq," *Weekly Standard,* February 2, 2004.

159. Daniel Williams, "Fallujah Insurgents Find a New Focus," *Washington Post,* February 8, 2004, p. A20.

160. Bradley Graham, "Huge Movement of Troops Is Underway," *Washington Post,* January 9, 2004, p. 13; Jim Krane, "Largest-Ever American Troop Rotation Is Under Way," *Miami Herald,* February 24, 2004; and, Thom Shanker, "U.S. Commanders Keep Their Guard Up as Forces Move," *New York Times.* February 29, 2004; and, Ann Scott Tyson, "Major Iraq Troop Rotation Gets Under Way," *Christian Science Monitor,* February 3, 2004, p. 1.

161. Liz Spayd and Thomas E. Ricks, "Rotation to Cut U.S. Presence," *Washington Post,* January 18, 2004, p. A17; and, Dan Murphy, "US To Begin Drawdown in Iraq," *Christian Science Monitor,* January 15, 2004, p. 1.

162. Thom Shanker, "Army Says Troop Rotation Into Iraq Poses Increased Danger," *New York Times,* November 26, 2003.

163. Vernon Loeb, "Army Reserve Chief Fears Retention Crisis," *Washington Post,* January 21, 2004, p. A4; and, Bradley Graham, "Army Cites Burdens Posed by Rotation," *Washington Post,* November 20, 2003, p. A39.

164. Esther Schrader, "Major Iraq Troop Rotation Begins," *Los Angeles Times,* January 9, 2004, p. A5; and Thom Shanker, "G.I.'s Heading For Iraq Train For Peace as Well as War," *New York Times,* January 20, 2004.

165. Lieutenant General Peter W. Chiarelli, commander Multinational Corps-Iraq, email correspondence to the author, October 6, 2006.

166. Thomas E. Ricks, "Soldiers Record Lessons From Iraq," *Washington Post,* February 8, 2004, p. A1; and Leon Shane III, "Army Steps Up Efforts to Monitor Military Bloggers," *Mideast Stars and Stripes,* October 29, 2006.

167. Leonard Wong, *Developing Adaptive Leaders: The Crucible Experience of Operation Iraqi Freedom,* Carlisle Barracks, PA: Strategic Studies Institute, U.S. Army War College, 2004, p. 15.

168. Major General George R. Fay, AR 15-6 Investigation of the Abu Ghraib Detention Facility And 205th Military Intelligence Brigade, August 23, 2004, p. 37.

169. Andrew Rathmell and David C. Gompert, "Iraq: Counter-Terrorism Strategy," action memo for the Administrator, Coalition Provisional Authority, Baghdad, March 13, 2004.

170. Coalition Provisional Authority English translation of terrorist Musab al Zarqawi letter obtained by United States Government in Iraq, February 2004. See also Dexter Filkins, "U.S. Says Files Seek Qaeda Aid In Iraq Conflict," *New York Times*, February 9, 2004, p. 1; Rowan Scarborough, "U.S. Adjusts to 'Changing' Tactics of Iraqi Rebels," *Washington Times*, March 8, 2004, p. 3.

171. John F. Burns, "At Least 143 Die in Attacks At Two Sacred Sites in Iraq," *New York Times*, March 3, 2004, p. 1; and Bradley Graham, "Deadly Attacks in Iraq Blamed on Zarqawi," *Washington Post*, March 4, 2004, p. A19.

172. For instance, Eric Schmitt, "U.S. Forces Rush to Send Tanks to Iraq," *New York Times*, April 29, 2004; Sharon Weinberger, "Military Sending 163 Robots to Iraq as 'Stopgap' Measure Against IEDs," *Defense Daily*, April 30, 2004, p. 4; Lisa Burgess, "Knowledge Is Power Against Roadside Bombs," *European Stars and Stripes*, April 26, 2004; and Steve Liewer, "Sandbags Become Makeshift Vehicle Armor," *European Stars and Stripes*, April 26, 2004.

173. Esther Schrader, "Tradition Left in the Dust as Army Reinvents Itself," *Los Angeles Times*, March 24, 2004, p. 1.

174. Stephen J. Hedges, "Military Learns Tough Lessons," *Chicago Tribune*, March 22, 2004; Rowan Scarborough, "U.S. Adjusts to 'Changing' Tactics of Iraqi Rebels," *Washington Times*, March 8, 2004, p. 3; Jeffrey Gettleman, "American Commanders Say That Keeping a Lower Profile in Baghdad Is Their Primary Goal," *New York Times*, February 10, 2004; Thom Shanker, "G.I.'s to Pull Back in Baghdad, Leaving Its Policing to Iraqis," *New York Times*, February 2, 2004; Brad Knickerbocker, "Military Might Tested, After the Battles," *Christian Science Monitor*, March 18, 2004; Thomas E. Ricks, "Marines to Offer New Tactics in Iraq," *Washington Post*, January 7, 2004, p. 1; and, Scott Wilson, "A Different Street Fight in Iraq," *Washington Post*, May 27, 2004, p. 1.

175. Peter W. Chiarelli and Patrick R. Michaelis, "Winning the Peace: The Requirement for Full-Spectrum Operations," *Military Review*, Vol. 85, No. 4, July-August 2005, pp. 4-17.

176. Quoted in Thom Shanker, "U.S. Prepares a Prolonged Drive to Suppress the Uprisings in Iraq," *New York Times*, April 11, 2004. Also, Ann Scott Tyson, "Insurgents In Iraq Show Signs of Acting As a Network," *Christian Science Monitor*, April 28, 2004; and Thomas E. Ricks, "Insurgents Display New Sophistication," *Washington Post*, April 14, 2004, p. A1.

177. "The Iraq War's New Phase," *Stratfor.com*, April 11, 2004.

178. Anthony Shadid, "U.S. Forces Take Heavy Losses as Violence Spreads Across Iraq," *Washington Post*, April 7, 2004, p. 1; Greg Jaffe and Michael M. Philips, "U.S. Troops Forced to Shift Gears in Iraq Fighting," *Wall Street Journal*, April 8, 2004, p. 4; Michael R. Gordon, "Iraq Insurgency Spreads, U.S. Finds More Foes and Fewer Friends," *New York Times*, April 9, 2004; Rajiv Chandrasekaran, "Anti-U.S. Uprising Widens in Iraq," *Washington Post*, April 8, 2004, p. A1; and, Michael Howard, "Insurgents Stir Up Strife in Kirkuk," *Washington Times*, May 17, 2004, p. 1.

179. Anthony Shadid and Sewell Chan, "Iraqi Militia Provokes More Clashes," *Washington Post*, April 6, 2004, p. A1; Greg Jaffe and Christopher Cooper, "Shiite Militants Post New Threat to U.S. In Iraq," *Wall Street Journal*, April 6, 2004, p. 1; Karl Vick and Sadd Sarhan, "Eight U.S. Troops Killed in Shiite Uprising," *Washington Post*, April 5, 2004, p. 1; John F. Burns, "7 U.S. Soldiers Die in Iraq as a Shiite Militia Rises Up," *New York Times*, April 5, 2004, p. 1; and, Anthony Shadid and Sewell Chan, "Protests Unleashed by Cleric Mark a New Front in War," *Washington Post*, April 5, 2004, p. A1.

180. Jeffrey Gettleman and Douglas Jehl, "Fierce Fighting With Sunnis and Shiites Spreads to 6 Iraqi Cities," *New York Times*, April 7, 2004, p.1.

181. Pamela Constable, "Marines, Insurgents Battle For Sunni City," *Washington Post*, April 8, 2004, p. 10; Karl Vick and Sewell Chan, "U.S. Troops Battle to Retake Cities," *Washington Post*, April 10, 2004, p. A1; West, No True Glory, pp. 53-220.

182. Karl Vick, "Shiite Rally To Sunni 'Brothers'," *Washington Post*, April 9, 2004, p. 1.

183. Bremer, *My Year In Iraq*, pp. 326-346; Jeffrey Gettleman, "Signs That Shiites and Sunnis Are Joining to Fight Americans,"

*New York Times*, April 9, 2004, p. 1; and, Annia Ciezadl, "Shi'ites Ally With Sunnis In Iraq," *Washington Times*, April 20, 2004, p. 12.

184. Rajiv Chandrasekaran, "Marines Plan Handoff to Militia in Fallujah," *Washington Post*, April 30, 2004, p. 1; and, Alissa J. Rubin, "Ineffective Iraqi Force in Fallouja Disbanded," *Los Angeles Times*, September 11, 2004, p. 1.

185. Bryan Bender, "Fallujah Insurgents Remain a Threat," *Boston Globe*, May 16, 2004.

186. Scott Wilson, "Over 60 Days, Troops Suppressed an Uprising," *Washington Post*, June 26, 2004, p. A1; Thom Shanker and Eric Schmitt, "Army Used Speed and Might, Plus Cash, Against Shiite Rebels," *New York Times*, June 26, 2004; Laura King, "Insurgents and Islam Now Rulers of Fallouja," *Los Angeles Times*, June 13, 2004, p. 1; Hashim, *Insurgency and Counter-Insurgency in Iraq*, pp. 43-44.

187. P. Mitchell Prothero, "Foreign Fighters Increase Presence in Iraq," *UPI.com*, June 23, 2004.

188. "Al Fallujah: Bed of Insurgency," *Stratfor.com*, July 9, 2004; and, John F. Burns and Erik Eckholm, "In Western Iraq, Fundamentalists Hold U.S. at Bay," *New York Times*, August 29, 2004, p. 1.

189. Anthony H. Cordesman, *The Implications of the Current Fighting in Iraq*, working paper, Washington, DC: Center for Strategic and International Studies, April 8, 2004, p. 5.

190. Karl Vick and Anthony Shadid, "Fallujah Gains Mythic Air," *Washington Post*, April 13, 2003, p. A1.

191. Jeffrey Fleishman, "Rumors Thrive in a Nation Shaped By Myth," *Los Angeles Times*, April 27, 2004.

192. Jeffrey Gettleman, "Anti-U.S. Outrage Unites a Growing Iraqi Resistance," *New York Times*, April 11, 2004; and, Farnaz Fassihi, "Iraqis Increasingly Sympathize With Rebels," *Wall Street Journal*, April 12, 2004, p. 16.

193. Dan Murphy, "Siege of Fallujah Polarizing Iraqis," *Christian Science Monitor*, April 15, 2004, p. 1.

194. Ken Dilanian, "Week's Violence Casts Doubt on Iraq Strategy," *Philadelphia Inquirer*, April 9, 2004, p. 1; and Brad Knickerbocker, "US Options in Dealing With a Widening War," *Christian Science Monitor*, April 9, 2004.

195. Robin Wright and Thomas E. Ricks, "U.S. Faces Growing Fears of Failure," *Washington Post*, May 19, 2004, p. 1.

196. Rowan Scarborough, "More Troops Needed For Iraq Occupation," *Washington Times*, April 10, 2004, p. 1.

197. Robert Burns, "Army Units Facing Quick Return to Iraq," *Miami Herald*, March 13, 2004; Douglas Jehl, Eric Schmitt, and David E. Sanger, "U.S. May Delay Departure of Some Troops in Iraq," *New York Times*, April 8, 2004; Eric Schmitt, "Army Extending Service For G.I.'s Due in War Zones," *New York Times*, June 3, 2004, p. 1; and Robert Burns, "Call For More Troops Could Be Tough on Army," *Philadelphia Inquirer*, April 29, 2004.

198. Rowan Scarborough, "Army Divisions Hit Re-Up Targets," *Washington Times*, April 2, 2004, p. 1; Harry Levins, "Army Sees Little Sign of Retention Crisis," *St. Louis Post-Dispatch*, April 7, 2004; Greg Jaffe, "Army Seeks Ways to Bolster Force in Iraq," *Wall Street Journal*, April 26, 2004, p. 4; Dan Fesperman, "Army Hopes It Has Enough in Reserve," *Baltimore Sun*, April 21, 2004; Rowan Scarborough, "Wars Causing Shortage of Officers," *Washington Times*, July 12, 2004, p. 1; Thomas E. Ricks and Josh White, "Fewer Army Recruits Lined Up," *Washington Post*, July 22, 2004, p. 2; Rowan Scarborough, "Army Meeting Recruiting Goal," *Washington Times*, July 27, 2004, p. 3; Thom Shanker, "Reserve System Needs Change, Military Experts Believe," *New York Times*, July 4, 2004; Esther Schrader, "Guard to Miss Its Recruiting Target," *Los Angeles Times*, September 24, 2004; and, Robert Burns, "Recruiting Gets Harder For Guard," *Philadelphia Inquirer*, September 24, 2005.

199. Vernon Loeb, "Army Will Face Dip in Readiness," *Washington Post*, December 6, 2003, p. A1; Esther Schrader, "Far From Ready For More War," *Los Angeles Times*, May 15, 2004, p. 1; and Stephen J. Hedges, "Insurgents' Escalation Taxing U.S. Capabilities," *Chicago Tribune*, April 24, 2004, p. 1.

200. Jonathan Karp and Greg Jaffe, "Army Plans to Postpone Modernization Program," *Wall Street Journal*, July 14, 2004, p. 7; and, Esther Schrader, "Iraq Conflict Disrupts U.S. Plans For Military," *Los Angeles Times*, June 15, 2004, p. 1.

201. Esther Schrader, "Army Says It Has Enough Troops For Three More Years," *Los Angeles Times*, June 16, 2004.

202. Quoted in Ann Scott Tyson, "Two Years Later, Iraq War Drains Military," *Washington Post*, March 19, 2005, p. 1.

203. Operational update briefing via teleconference between Baghdad, Iraq, and the Pentagon, April 12, 2004. The ICDC was considered a failure and was later renamed the National Guard and merged into the regular army.

204. Thomas E. Ricks, "Petraeus To Get Key Job in Iraq," *Washington Post*, April 3, 2004, p. 20; Eric Schmitt and Thom Shanker, "Training Skills of U.S. General Sought After Poor Performance by Some Iraqi Forces," *New York Times*, April 15, 2004; Dexter Filkins, "Biggest Task for U.S. General Is Training Iraqis to Fight Iraqis," *New York Times*, June 27, 2004; and Rod Nordland, "Iraq's Repairman," *Newsweek*, July 5, 2004.

205. Bremer, *My Year in Iraq*, pp. 274-275; and, Chandrasekaran, *Imperial Life in the Emerald City*, 255-256.

206. Ricks, *Fiasco*, p. 371.

207. Quoted in Scott Wilson, "From Occupation to 'Partnership'," *Washington Post*, June 29, 2004, p. 19.

208. Ed Timms, "U.S. Troops Shifting from Enforcer to Reinforcer," *Dallas Morning News*, July 11, 2004; Bradley Graham, "U.S. Forces Plan Lower Profile," *Washington Post*, June 21, 2004, p. 15; Thom Shanker, "U.S. Shifts Focus in Iraq to Aiding New Government," *New York Times*, June 1, 2004, p. 1; Tom Bowman, "For U.S. Soldiers on the Ground, the Handover Yields a Supporting Role," *Baltimore Sun*, June 27, 2004; and, Thanassis Cambanis, "US Troops See Duties Expand Beyond Security," *Boston Globe*, July 5, 2004, p. 1.

209. Thomas E. Ricks, "Counterinsurgency Academy Giving Officers a New Mind-Set," *Washington Post*, February 21, 2006, p. A10.

210. General John P. Abizaid, testimony before the Senate Armed Services Committee, Washington, DC, March 1, 2005.

211. Robin Wright, "State Department Now Assumes a Greater Role," *Washington Post*, June 29, 2004, p. 16.

212. Tom Lasseter, "Wary U.S. Troops End Patrols in Iraqi Area," *Philadelphia Inquirer*, July 21, 2004, p. 1.

213. Jeffrey Gettelman, "Attacks in 5 Iraqi Cities Leave More Than 100 Dead," *New York Times*, June 25, 2004, p. 1; and, Doug Struck, "Dozens of Iraqis Die in Violence in 3 Cities," *Washington Post*, June 27, 2004, p. A18. The security situation in the north had eroded since the spring of 2004, in large part because Task Force

Olympia had fewer resources, particularly intelligence assets, than the 101st Airborne which it replaced.

214. Edward Cody, "Foes of U.S. in Iraq Criticize Insurgents," *Washington Post*, June 26, 2004, p. A1.

215. Karl Vick, "Insurgents Massacre 49 Iraqi Recruits," *Washington Post*, October 25, 2004, p.A1; Edward Wong, "Ambush Kills 50 Iraqi Soldiers Execution Style," *New York Times*, October 25, 2004, p. A.

216. Eric Schmitt and Steven R. Weisman, "U.S. Conceding Rebels Control Region of Iraq," *New York Times*, September 8, 2004, p. 1; and Steven Komarow, Csar G. Soriano, and Tom Squitieri, "Insurgents in Iraq Appear More Powerful Than Ever," *USA Today*, September 16, 2004, p. 1.

217. Tom Bowman, "U.S. May Soon Have to Pacify Iraq's Cities," *Baltimore Sun*, September 9, 2004.

218. See West, *No True Glory*, pp. 255-316.

219. Robert F. Worth and James Glanz, "U.S. Presses Fight in Falluja: Insurgents Strike Other Cities," *New York Times*, November 12, 2004, p. 1; Karl Vick and Bassam Sebti, "Violence Erupts Across Iraq at Sites Far From Fallujah," *Washington Post*, November 12, 2004, p. A21; Alissa J. Rubin and Tyler Marshall, "Beyond Embattled City, Rebels Operate Freely," *Los Angeles Times*, November 12, 2004, p. 1; Borzou Daraghi, "U.S. Forces Launch Attacks on Militants in Mosul," *Washington Times*, November 12, 2004, p. 15; Karl Vick and Jackie Spinner, "Insurgent Attacks Spread in Iraq," *Washington Post*, November 16, 2004, p. A1; Karl Vick, "Trouble Spots Dot Iraqi Landscape," *Washington Post*, November 15, 2004, p. A1; Dexter Filkins and James Glanz, "Rebels Routed in Falluja: Fighting Spreads Elsewhere in Iraq," *New York Times*, November 15, 2004, p. 1; Edward Wong, "Showing Their Resolve, Rebels Mount Attacks in Northern and Central Iraq," *New York Times*, November 18, 2004, p. 1.

220. "Iraq Insurgents Stir Sectarian Violence," *Baltimore Sun*, November 21, 2004; Maggie Michael, "Terrorist Militia Claims Mosul Slaughter," *Washington Times*, November 29, 2004, p. 14; Robert F. Worth and Richard A. Oppel, Jr., "27 Civilians Die in New Attacks by Iraqi Rebels," *New York Times*, December 4, 2004; Anthony Shadid and Karl Vick, "Ethnic Violence Kills Dozens in Iraq," *Washington Post*, December 5, 2004, p. A1; and, Robert F. Worth and Richard A. Oppel, Jr., "Insurgents' Attacks Kill at least 26 Iraqis," *New York Times*, December 5, 2004.

221. Ian Fisher and Edward Wong, "Iraq's Rebellion Develops Signs of Internal Rift," *New York Times*, July 11, 2004, p. 1; Dan Murphy, "Iraqi Rebels Dividing, Losing Support," *Christian Science Monitor*, July 12, 2004, p. 1; Karl Vick, "Insurgent Alliance Is Fraying in Fallujah," *Washington Post*, October 13, 2004, p. 1; Hannah Allam, "Backlash Against Fallujah Outsiders," *Philadelphia Inquirer*, November 14, 2004, p. 1; Hamza Hendawi, "Insurgents Show Hostility to Extremists," *San Diego Union-Tribune*, April 10, 2005; Sabrina Tavernise, "Marines See Signs Iraq Rebels Are Battling Foreign Fighters," *New York Times*, June 21, 2005; Ellen Knickmeyer and Jonathan Finer, "Iraqi Sunnis Battle to Defend Shiites," *Washington Post*, August 14, 2005, p. A1; and, Mohammed Al Dulaimy, "Al-Qai'da in Iraq Fights Other Terrorist Groups," *Detroit Free Press*, November 10, 2005.

222. Erik Eckholm, "Sunni Group Say It Killed Cleric's Aide in Bombing," *New York Times*, January 15, 2005; and, Anthony Shadid, "Sunni Group Says It Killed Shiite Cleric," *Washington Post*, January 14, 2004, p. A14.

223. Doug Struck and Bassam Sebti, "30 Killed in Iraq on Shiite Holy Day," *Washington Post*, February 19, 2005, p. A1.

224. Sabrina Tavernise and Robert F. Worth, "Relentless Rebel Attacks Test Shiite Endurance," *New York Times*, September 19, 2005, p. 1.

225. For instance, Robert F. Worth, "Iraqi Civilians Fight Back Against Insurgents," *New York Times*, March 23, 2005; Sabrina Tavernise, "Many Iraqis See Sectarian Roots in New Killings," *New York Times*, May 27, 2005, p. 1; Yochi J. Dreazen, "Shiites" Better Safe Than Sorry," *Wall Street Journal*, July 26, 2005, p. 10; and, James Hider and Ali Hamdani, "Sectarian Slaughter Sets Iraq on Road to Schism," *London Times*, February 28, 2006.

226. *The Next Iraqi War?* p. 1.

227. Abizaid, testimony before the Senate Armed Services Committee, March 1, 2005.

228. Doug Struck, "Iraqis Cite Shift in Attitudes Since Vote," *Washington Post*, February 7, 2005, p. A1; and, Rowan Scarborough, "Elections Prompt Iraq Insurgents to Question Fight," *Washington Times*, February 23, 2005, p. 6.

229. Rowan Scarborough, "Pentagon Begins to See Iraq Momentum Shift," *Washington Times*, March 28, 2005, p. 1; Bill Gertz, "Myers Says U.S. Winning in Iraq," *Washington Times*,

April 27, 2005, p. 6; Mark Mazzetti, "Insurgency Is Waning, a Top U.S. General Says," *Los Angeles Times*, March 2, 2005, p. A7; The Beginning of the End for Sunni Insurgents? *Stratfor.com*, April 1, 2005; and Vice President Dick Cheney, interviewed on CNN's Larry King Live, June 20, 2005.

230. Edward Wong, "25 Killed as Insurgents in Iraq Carry Out a Wave of Attacks," *New York Times*, February 25, 2005; Caryle Murphy, "Zarqawi's Group Says It Was Behind Attack," *Washington Post*, March 2, 2005, p. A12; Mark Mazzetti and Solomon Moore, "Insurgents Flourish in Iraq's Wild West," *Los Angeles Times*, May 24, 2005; Dexter Filkins and David S. Cloud, "Defying U.S. Efforts, Guerrillas in Iraq Refocus and Strengthen," *New York Times*, July 24, 2005, p. 1; Tom Lasseter, "Insurgents Have Changed U.S. Ideas About Winning," *Philadelphia Inquirer*, August 28, 2005, p. 1; and Ellen Knickmeyer and Jonathan Finer, "Insurgents Assert Control Over Town Near Syrian Border," *Washington Post*, September 6, 2005, p. A20.

231. Pamela Hess, "Insurgents Regain Foothold, Unleash Terror in Fallujah," *Washington Times*, September 1, 2005, p. 1.

232. Eric Schmitt, "U.S. and Allies Capture More Foreign Fighters," *New York Times*, June 19, 2005; Bryan Bender, "Study Cites Seeds of Terror in Iraq," *Boston Globe*, July 17, 2005, p. 1; Anthony H. Cordesman, *Iraq and Foreign Volunteers*, Washington, DC: Center for Strategic and International Studies, 2005; and, Nawaf Obaid and Anthony Cordesman, *Saudi Militants in Iraq: Assessment and the Kingdom's Response*, Washington, DC: Center for Strategic and International Studies, 2005.

233. Major General Richard Zahner, quoted in Bradley Graham, "Zarqawi 'Hijacked' Insurgency," *Washington Post*, September 28, 2005, p. A17.

234. Carol. J. Williams, "Suicide Attacks Rising Rapidly," *Los Angeles Times*, June 2, 2005, p. 1.

235. John Hendren, "Rebels Banking on U.S. Pullout, Official Says," *Los Angeles Times*, July 23, 2005.

236. *In Their Own Words*, p. 14.

237. Thom Shanker, "Pentagon Says Iraq Efforts Limits Ability to Fight Other Conflicts," *New York Times*, May 3, 2005, p. 1; Josh White and Ann Scott Tyson, "Wars Strain U.S. Military Capability, Pentagon Reports," *Washington Post*, May 3, 2005, p. 6.

238. Ann Scott Tyson, "Recruiting Shortfall Delays Army's Expansion Plans," *Washington Post*, October 4, 2005, p. 7; Mark Mazzetti, "Army Plans to Reorganize, Not Expand, to Meet Combat Needs," *Los Angeles Times*, October 7, 2005; and, Ann Scott Tyson, "Army Reorganizes to Boost Its Combat Power," *Washington Post*, October 7, 2005, p. 2.

239. Brad Knickerbocker, "As Iraq Effort Drags On, Doubts Mount at Home," *Christian Science Monitor*, June 17, 2005, p. 1; Bryan Bender, "US General Says Troops Question Support," *Boston Globe*, June 24, 2005, p. 1.

240. Tom Lasseter, "Officers: Military Can't End Insurgency," *Philadelphia Inquirer*, June 13, 2005, p. 1; and, Thomas E. Ricks, "Dissension Grows in Senior Ranks on War Strategy," *Washington Post*, May 9, 2005, p. 1.

241. Ellen Knickmeyer and Caryle Murphy, "U.S. Ends Iraqi Border Offensive," *Washington Post*, May 15, 2005, p. 24; Mohammed Barakat, "Military Suspends Offensive in Iraq," *Washington Times*, May 15, 2005, p. 1; Tom Lasseter, "Officers Say Army Lacks Troops to Protect Gains," *Miami Herald*, June 1, 2005, p. 1; Patrick J. McDonnell, "U.S., Iraq Launch Large Assault on Insurgents Near Border With Syria," *Los Angeles Times*, June 18, 2005; James Glanz, "U.S. Troops Begin New Offensive in Iraqi Desert Near Syrian Border," *New York Times*, June 18, 2005; and Dan Murphy, "US Strategy in Iraq: Is It Working?" *Christian Science Monitor*, June 21, 2005, p. 1.

242. Tom Lasseter, "Insurgents Have Changed U.S. Ideas About Winning," *Philadelphia Inquirer*, August 28, 2005, p. 1.

243. Ricks, *Fiasco*, pp. 419-421; and, George Packer, "Letter From Iraq: The Lessons of Tal Afar," *New Yorker*, April 10, 2006.

244. Mark Sappenfield, "US Tempers Its View of Victory in Iraq," *Christian Science Monitor*, September 16, 2005, p. 1; David Ignatius, "A Shift on Iraq," *Washington Post*, September 26, 2005, p. 23; Solomon Moore, "U.S. Is Ceding More Control to Iraqis," *Los Angeles Times*, October 29, 2005, p. 1; and, Eric Schmitt, "U.S. to Intensify Its Training in Iraq to Battle Insurgents," *New York Times*, November 2, 2005.

245. Testimony before the Senate Armed Services Committee, Washington, DC, September 29, 2005.

246. Secretary of State Condoleezza Rice, "Iraq and U.S. Policy," testimony before the Senate Committee on Foreign Relations, October 19, 2005.

247. President Bush discusses war on terror following Pentagon briefing, January 4, 2006.

248. Elaine M. Grossman, "New Bush Strategy in Iraq Will Aim to Shield Public From Insurgents," *Inside the Pentagon*, November 3, 2005, p. 1; Scott Peterson, "New Iraq Strategy: Stay in Hot Spots," *Christian Science Monitor*, November 23, 2005, p. 1; Kirk Semple, "U.S. Forces Try New Approach: Raid and Dig In," *New York Times*, December 5, 2005, p. 1; and, Bradley Graham, "Calls For Shift in Iraq Strategy Growing," *Washington Post*, November 11, 2005, p. 16. Anbar was the testbed of the new approach. See John Ward Anderson, "U.S. and Iraqi Forces Open Major Assault," *Washington Post*, November 6, 2005, p. 23; John Ward Anderson, "U.S. Widens Offensive in Far Western Iraq," *Washington Post*, November 15, 2005, p. 16; Kirk Semple, "U.S.-Iraq Force Presses Sweep Against Rebels," *New York Times*, December 2, 2005; and Colonel H.R. McMaster, commander of the 3rd Armored Cavalry Regiment, video news briefing, January 27, 2006. One of the most persuasive and rigorous treatments of the need for pacification appeared in Andrew F. Krepinevich Jr., "How to Win in Iraq," *Foreign Affairs*, Vol. 84, No. 5, September/October 2005, pp. 87-104.

249. *National Strategy for Victory in Iraq*, Washington, DC: National Security Council, p. 3. Emphasis added.

250. David E. Sanger, "Administration's Tone Signals a Longer, Broader Iraq Conflict," *New York Times*, October 17, 2005.

251. *National Strategy for Victory in Iraq*, p. 4.

252. General Richard B. Myers, Chairman of the Joint Chiefs of Staff, testimony before the Senate Armed Services Committee, Washington, DC, September 29, 2005.

253. Thomas E. Ricks, "In the Battle for Baghdad, U.S. Turns War on Insurgents," *Washington Post*, February 26, 2006, p. 1.

254. Quoted in Nelson Hernandez and Saad al-Izzi, "Iraqi President Says Sunni Insurgents See Iran as Threat," *Washington Post*, May 3, 2006, p. 14.

255. Richard A. Oppel, Jr., "Up to 130 Killed in Iraq, Drawing a Shiite Warning," *New York Times*, January 6, 2006, p. 1; Nelson Hernandez and Saad Sarhan, "Insurgents Kill 140 as Iraq Clashes Escalate," *Washington Post*, January 6, 2006, p. A1; Anna Badkhen, "Militants Revive Cycle of Violence," *San Francisco Chronicle*, January 10, 2006, p. 1; and Ellen Knickmeyer and Bassam Sebti,

"Toll in Iraq's Deadly Surge: 1,300," *Washington Post*, February 28, 2006, p. A1.

256. Anthony H. Cordesman, *Iraq's Evolving Insurgency and the Risk of Civil War*, Washington, DC: Center for Strategic and International Studies, 2006, pp. 210-211; and Dan Murphy, "Death Squads Deepen Division in Baghdad," *Christian Science Monitor*, May 8, 2006.

257. Sabrina Tavernise, "Alarmed By Raids, Neighbors Stand Guard in Iraq," *New York Times*, May 10, 2006, p. 1.

258. *Iraq's Evolving Insurgency and the Risk of Civil War*, April 2006, pp. 47-49; Sharon Behn, "Iraqis Driven From Homes to Desperation By Militias," *Washington Times*, April 20, 2006, p. 16; and Richard A. Oppel, Jr., "100,000 Families Are Fleeing Violence," *New York Times*, April 30, 2006, p. 1.

259. Oliver Poole, "Mobs Cheer British Deaths as Basra Slips Out of Control," *London Daily Telegraph*, May 8, 2006.

260. Jeffrey Fleishman, "A Threat That Tops Insurgency," *Los Angeles Times*, August 27, 2006, p. 1.

261. Sudarsan Raghavan, "Militias Splintering Into Radicalized Cells," *Washington Post*, October 19, 2006, p. 1.

262. *Measuring Stability and Security in Iraq: Report to Congress*, August 2006, p. 26.

263. Solomon Moore and Louise Roug, "Deaths Across Iraq Show It is a Nation of Many Wars, With U.S. in the Middle," *Los Angles Times*, October 7, 2006, p. 1.

264. Anthony Shadid, "This Is Baghdad: What Could Be Worse?" *Washington Post*, October 29, 2006, p. B1.

265. Thomas E. Ricks, "Situation Called Dire in West Iraq," *Washington Post*, September 11, 2006, p. 1; Thomas E. Ricks, "General Affirms Anbar Analysis, " *Washington Post*, September 13, 2006, p. 12; Michael R. Gordon, "Grim Report Out of Anbar Is Disputed by General," *New York Times*, September 13, 2006; and Ann Scott Tyson, "Pentagon Weighing Report on Anbar," *Washington Post*, September 12, 2006, p. 19.

266. Colonel Robert Scurlock, video news briefing from Baghdad, August 25, 2006. See also Dexter Filkins and Qais Mizher, "Baghdad's Chaos Undercuts Tack Pursued By U.S.," *New York Times*, August 6, 2006, p. 1; Patrick J. McDonnell and Louise

Roug, "A New Offensive, An Old Conundrum," *Los Angeles Times*, August 30, 2006, p. A8; Solomon Moore, "U.S. Fatalities in Iraq Rise Amid Crackdown," *Los Angeles Times*, October 4, 2006; Amit R. Paley, "Attacks In Baghdad Kill 13 U.S. Soldiers In 3 Days," *Washington Post*, October 5, 2006, p. 1; and Patrick Quinn, "A Must Win Battle," *Philadelphia Inquirer*, October 6, 2006

267. Michael R. Gordon, "To Stand or Fall in Baghdad: Capital is Key to Mission," *New York Times*, October 23, 2006, p. 1.

268. Antonio Castaneda, "U.S. Focusing Energy, Troops on Baghdad," *Houston Chronicle*, October 10, 2006.

269. Christopher Bodeen, "Talks in Iraq Are Delayed as 86 Killed," *Philadelphia Inquirer*, October 16, 2006.

270. David S. Cloud, "Top U.S. Officer in Iraq Sees Spike in Violence," *New York Times*, October 12, 2006.

271. John F. Burns, "General Weighs 2d Troop Shift to Calm Baghdad," *New York Times*, October 25, 2006, p. 1; and Ellen Knickmeyer, "More U.S. Troops May Be Iraq-Bound," *Washington Post*, October 25, 2006, p. 1.

272. Greg Jaffe, "Problems Afflict U.S. Program to Advise Iraqis," *Wall Street Journal*, October 18, 2006, p. 1; and Max Boot, "Bring Iraqi Forces Up to Speed," *Los Angeles Times*, October 18, 2006.

273. James Fallows, "Why Iraq Has No Army," *Atlantic Monthly*, December 2005, pp. 60-77; Thomas E. Ricks, "U.S. Military Is Still Waiting For Iraqi Forces to 'Stand Up'," *Washington Post*, October 1, 2006, p. 21; and Solomon Moore and Julian E. Barnes, "Many Iraqi Troops Are No-Shows in Baghdad," *Los Angeles Times*, September 23, 2006, p. 1. For analysis, see Anthony H. Cordesman, *Iraqi Force Development and the Challenge of Civil War: Can Iraqi Forces Do the Job?* Washington, DC: Center for Strategic and International Studies, 2006; and David M. Walker, Comptroller General of the United States, *Stabilizing Iraq: An Assessment of the Security Situation*, testimony for the Subcommittee on National Security, Emerging Threats and International Relations, House Committee on Government Reform, Washington, DC: General Accounting Office, September 11, 2006.

274. Brigadier General Dana Pittard, video news conference from Baghdad, August 28, 2006.

275. Antonio Castaneda, "U.S. Soldiers See Inept Output By Iraqi Troops," *Washington Times*, September 25, 2006, p. 1.

276. Amit R. Paley, "In Baghdad, a Force Under the Militias' Sway," *Washington Post*, October 31, 2006, p. 1.

277. Charles J. Hanley, "Much of Iraq Still in Ruins as U.S. Builders Leave," *Houston Chronicle*, October 15, 2006; and Griff Witte, "Auditors Say Shift of Rebuilding to Iraqis Appears 'Broken Down'," *Washington Post*, October 31, 2006, p. 17.

278. Michael Abramowltz and Thomas E. Ricks, "Ability of New Iraqi Leaders Doubted," *Washington Post*, October 13, 2006, p. 11; and Rowan Scarborough, "Iraqi Forces Concern U.S. Commander," *Washington Times*, October 16, 2006, p. 1.

279. James Lyons, "Multifaceted Strategy for Iraq," *Washington Times*, October 16, 2006, p. 19.

280. John Ward Anderson, "General Says Mission in Baghdad Falls Short," *Washington Post*, October 20, 2006, p. 1; and John F. Burns, "U.S. Says Violence in Baghdad Rises, Foiling Campaign," *New York Times*, October 20, 2006, p. 1.

281. John Ward Anderson, "Sadr Militia Briefly Seizes Southern City," *Washington Post*, October 21, 2006, p. 13; and Kirk Semple, "Militias Battle for Iraqi City as Shiite Rivalry Escalates," *New York Times*, October 21, 2006, p. 1.

282. Amit R. Paley, "Most Iraqis Favor Immediate U.S. Pullout, Polls Show," *Washington Post*, September 27, 2006, p. 22; and "Polls Show Most Iraqis Want U.S. Out," *New York Times*, September 29, 2006.

283. CNN Poll conducted by Opinion Research Corporation. Sept. 22-24, 2006.

284. Gallup News Service, October 13, 2006.

285. Sheryl Gay Stolberg, "Warner's Remarks Surprise White House," *New York Times*, October 7, 2006.

286. Quoted in Allen Cowell, "Top General Urges Britain to Leave Iraq," *New York Times*, October 13, 2006. Also, "British General Calls for Pullout 'Soon' From Iraq," *Washington Post*, October 13, 2006, p. A23.

287. Thom Shanker, "Army and Other Ground Forces Meet '06 Recruiting Goals," *New York Times*, October 10, 2006, p. 19; and Lynn E. Davis, et. al., *Stretched Thin: Army Forces For Sustained Operations*, Santa Monica, CA: RAND Corporation, 2005.

288. Quoted in David Wood, "Warfare Skills Eroding as Army Fights Insurgents," *Baltimore Sun*, October 24, 2006.

289. Peter Spiegel, "Army Warns Rumsfeld It's Billions Short," *Los Angeles Times*, September 25, 2006, p. 1. There were indications that the Army would receive a larger proportion of the defense budget, and that the congressionally mandated increases in the Army's force size, which were intended to be temporary, may become at least long term (Thom Shanker and David S. Cloud, "Rumsfeld Shift Lets Army Seek Larger Budget," *New York Times*, October 8, 2006). Eventually Deputy Secretary of Defense Gordon England directed a $7 billion increase in the Army's fiscal year 2008 budget but that was $17.8 billion short of what service leaders requested. (Jason Sherman, "England Directs $7 Billion Increase to Army's FY-08 Budget Request," *Inside the Pentagon*, October 26, 2006, p. 1; and David S. Cloud, "White House Is Trimming Army Budget for Next Year, Officials Say," *New York Times*, October 28, 2006, p. 16.)

290. For instance, Jeffrey Record, "Why America Keeps Losing 'Small Wars'," *Baltimore Sun*, October 15, 2006.

291. For instance, Rick Brennan, *et. al.*, *Future Insurgency Threats*, Santa Monica, CA: RAND Corporation, 2005; and David Kilcullen, "Countering Global Insurgency," *Journal of Strategic Studies*, Vol 28, No. 4, August 2005, pp. 597-617.

292. *National Defense Strategy of the United States of America*, Washington, DC: Department of Defense, 2005, p. 3.

293. Briefing prepared by the Quadrennial Defense Review Irregular Warfare Study Group, May 23, 2005. The phrase "irregular warfare" was used in the *Quadrennial Defense Review* but did not appear in the *National Security Strategy of the United States of America* (2006), *The National Military Strategy Plan for the War on Terrorism* (2006), *National Strategy for Victory in Iraq* (2005), *National Strategy for Combating Terrorism* (2003), *National Defense Strategy of the United States of America* (2005), or *National Military Strategy of the United States of America* (2004). (Source: Irregular Warfare Special Study, Norfolk, VA: U.S. Joint Forces Command, 2006, pp. II-1 through II-2.)

294. See Greg Jaffe, "Rumsfeld Details Big Military Shift in New Document," *Wall Street Journal*, March 11, 2005, p. 1; Mark Mazzetti, "Iraq War Compels Pentagon to Rethink Big-Picture Strategy," *Los Angeles Times*, March 11, 2005, p. 1.

295. Antulio J. Echevarria II, *Toward an American Way of War*, Carlisle Barracks, PA: Strategic Studies Institute, U.S. Army War College, 2004.

296. Department of Defense Directive 3000.05, "Military Support for Stability, Security, Transition, and Reconstruction Operations," November 28, 2005. For analysis, see Rowan Scarborough, "Nation-Building Elevated," *Washington Times*, December 14, 2005, p. 1; Thom Shanker and David S. Cloud, "Pentagon to Raise Importance of 'Stability' Efforts in War," *New York Times*, November 20, 2005; Bradley Graham, "U.S. Directive Prioritizes Post-Conflict Stability," *Washington Post*, December 1, 2005, p. 21; Mark Sappenfield, "New Military Goals: 'Win the Peace'," *Christian Science Monitor*, December 16, 2005, p. 1; and, Neil King Jr. and Greg Jaffe, "U.S. Sets New Mission For Keeping the Peace," *Wall Street Journal*, January 3, 2006, p. 4.

297. See Rowan Scarborough, "New Pentagon Strategy Sees 'Long War' on Terror," *Washington Times*, February 4, 2006, p. 4; and, Ann Scott Tyson, "Ability to Wage 'Long War' Is Key to Pentagon Plan," *Washington Post*, February 4, 2006, p. 1.

298. *Quadrennial Defense Review Report*, Washington, DC: Department of Defense, 2006, p. 1.

299. *The National Security Strategy of the United States of America*, Washington, DC: The White House, 2006.

300. Bob Woodward reports that as late as November 2003, President Bush and Secretary Rumsfeld refused to call the conflict in Iran an insurgency. *State of Denial: Bush at War, Part III*, New York: Simon & Schuster, 2006, pp. 266-267.

301. Qiao Liang and Wang Xiangsui, *Unrestricted Warfare*, Beijing: PLA Literature and Arts Publishing House, 1999. Nathan Freier drew my attention to this similarity between unrestricted warfare and insurgency.

302. Ann Scott Tyson, "Crunch Time For Special Ops Forces," *Christian Science Monitor*, April 6, 2004; and, David Wood, "Special Forces Stretched Thin by Two Wars," *Baltimore Sun*, September 24, 2006, p. 1.

303. Ann Roosevelt, "SO/LIC Building Capability, Capacity for Irregular Warfare," *Defense Daily*, October 19, 2006; Ann Scott Tyson, "Plan Seeks More Elite Forces to Fortify Military," *Washington Post*, January 24, 2006, p. A1; and *Quadrennial Defense Review Report*, pp. 44-45.

304. *Quadrennial Defense Review Report*, p. 78. See also Rati Bishnoi, "DOD Kicks Off Program to Recruit, Train Critical Language Speakers," *Inside the Pentagon*, December 15, 2005, p. 1; Rowan Scarborough, "Military Planners Envision 'New Breed of Warrior'," *Washington Times*, January 31, 2006, p. 9; and, Mark Sappenfield, "What US Wants In Its Troops: Cultural Savvy," *Christian Science Monitor*, July 5, 2006, p. 1.

305. Thomas E. Ricks, "Lessons Learned In Iraq Show Up In Army Classes," *Washington Post*, January 21, 2006, p. 1. The Army War College added lessons on counterinsurgency to its core national security strategy and policy and theory of war and strategy courses. It also developed several elective courses that dealt wholly or partially with counterinsurgency. Email correspondence with Colonel Kevin Weddle, Deputy Dean for Academic Affairs, U.S. Army War College, Carlisle Barracks, PA, October 4, 2006.

306. Sandra I. Erwin, "Iraq Lessons Pervade Army War Games," *National Defense*, June 2005.

307. Lieutenant General James J. Lovelace, Jr. and Brigadier General Joseph L. Votel, "The Asymmetric Warfare Group: Closing the Capability Gaps," *Army*, March 2005, pp. 29-34.

308. Greg Jaffe, "Problems Afflict U.S. Army Program to Advise Iraqis," *Wall Street Journal*, October 18, 2006, p. 1; and Peter Spiegel, "Army Is Training Advisors for Iraq," *Los Angeles Times*, October 25, 2006, p.1.

309. Jacob Kipp, Lester Grau, Karl Prinslow, and Don Smith, "The Human Terrain System: a CORDS for the 21st Century," *Military Review*, Vol. 86, No. 5, September-October 2006, pp. 8-15.

310. Discussion with senior Army commander, October 7, 2006.

311. Bryan Bender, "US Testing Nonlethal Weapons Arsenal For Use in Iraq," *Boston Globe*, August 5, 2005; Steven Komarow, "Energy Beam Weapon May Lower Iraq Civilian Deaths," *USA Today*, July 25, 2005, p. 1; Steven Komarow, "Pentagon Deploys Array of Non-Lethal Weapons," *USA Today*, July 25, 2005, p. 14; Erich Schmitt, "U.S. Drones Crowding the Skies to Help Fight Insurgents in Iraq," *New York Times*, April 5, 2005; Shaun Waterman, "Military Seeks to Develop 'Insect Cyborgs'," *Washington Times*, March 13, 2006, p. 6; and, Robert S. Boyd, "Pentagon Works to Increase Its Army of Robots," *Miami Herald*, February 14, 2006.

312. FMI (Field Manual Interim) 3-07.22, *Counterinsurgency Operations*, October 2004.

313. Michael R. Gordon, "Military Hones a New Strategy on Counterinsurgency," *New York Times*, October 5, 2006, p. 1.

314. *A Concept for Distributed Operations*, Washington, DC, Headquarters, U.S. Marine Corps, 2005, p. I.

315. A draft was circulating in the late summer of 2006, but it was not approved and published as this monograph was completed.

316. Glenn Kessler, "Bush Names Rice to Head Nation Rebuilding," *Washington Post*, December 15, 2005, p. 31.

317. Ambassador Carlos Pascual, prepared statement for the Senate Foreign Relations Committee, June 16, 2005; and, "An Interview With Carlos Pascual, Vice President and Director of Foreign Policy Studies of the Brookings Institution," *Joint Force Quarterly*, Issue 42, 3d Quarter 2006, pp. 80-85.

318. Andrew S. Natsios, "The Nine Principles of Reconstruction and Development," *Parameters*, Vol. 35, No. 3, Autumn 2005, p. 4.

319. United States Agency for International Development, FY 2006 Annual Budget Submission.

320. In 2004, for instance, USAID approached the author about preparing a study of the nature of counterinsurgency and the role of USAID in it for the agency's senior managers.

321. Gordon McCormick, presentation to the RAND Insurgency Board, Arlington, VA, August 29, 2006. An article based on this paper will appear as "Things Fall Apart: The 'Endgame" Dynamics of Internal Wars," *Third World Quarterly*, Vol. 28, No. 2, 2007.

322. On the idea of counterinsurgency planning based on psychological effects, see in Metz and Millen, *Insurgency and Counterinsurgency in the 21st Century*, pp. 25-26.

323. John Nagl's *Learning to Eat Soup With a Knife* is the most rigorous study of how counterinsurgent organizations become (or do not become) "learning organizations."

324. Hans Binnendijk and Stuart E. Johnson, *Transforming for Stabilization and Reconstruction Operations*, Washington, DC: National Defense University Center for Technology and National Security Policy, 2004, pp. 53-69. This excellent study goes into some detail on what such an organization might look like. Thomas